Bipolar Party

Austin, Aspen or Beyond?

Ray Loyd Tune

chipmunkapublishing
the mental health publisher

Published by
Chipmunkapublishing
PO Box 6872
Brentwood
Essex CM13 1ZT
United Kingdom

http://www.chipmunkapublishing.com

Copyright © Ray Loyd Tune 2012

Edited by Duke D. Pennell / Aleks Lech

ISBN   978-1-84991-754-4

Chipmunkapublishing   gratefully   acknowledge   the support of Arts Council England.

The experiences recorded in this book are factual; some names have been changed, for obvious reasons. The setting is rooted primarily in Austin, Aspen, Dallas and Houston, from the 1960's through to the 1990's; as such, it is dated. Due to the latent manifestation of bipolar disorder, it took forty years for me to fully understand and acknowledge the nature of my mental disconnect.

My book is intended for men and women who, although are functioning members of society, just don't feel like they fit in. Many are quite successful; even over-achievers. Others may experience bouts of depression. The one central theme the reader should take away is that it is never too late to seek professional help. Don't waste your life feeding the disorder; begin treatment while you're young.

The Author
Fayetteville, AR 2011

Where Do I Belong?

ACKNOWLEDGMENTS

There are simply too many friends, professionals, and supporters to mention by name. My ex-wives who each gave me their love and assistance. Leigh who assisted me with my memory and my English grammar - thanks. Jill, my first wife was and still is one of my best friends, she has one of the best senses of humor of anyone on earth (must have, she married me). Annie Maria was and still is an adorable, intelligent and fun person to be around, she was the first to insist I see a doctor about my emotional issues.

No child in this world should have to endure what I must have put them through. Steven, Krisi, Kelsey, Robert and my youngest son, Garrett, are the loves of my life. But for them, I would surely have been institutionalized.

A gigantic hug to Duke Pennell, my editor and mentor, and Patricia Lockwood, my loving Christian friend from Ft. Smith who gave so much of her time in perfecting the cover jackets.

Last but not least are three of my mental health providers and/or friends:
       Dr. Jeff Jenkins, MD Psychiatrist – Stilwell, OK
       Dr. Patricia Hill, PhD, Psychologist – Aspen, CO
       Dr. Mooney, MD, Psychiatrist, VA Medical, Fayetteville, AR

Where Do I Belong?

Preface

As a child, I helped my grandparents tend the garden, harvest corn, and milk and feed critters. Every day was a milk day, the old cows didn't take holidays or vacations; they had to be milked twice a day, every day, same time, morning and night. Of course, I always found time during the day for hunting and fishing, mostly fishing; I liked dangling my feet in the water and teasing the turtles.

My mother remarried when I was seven and I moved from my little Walden to a rather large farm with fifty head of milk cows—all of which were milked twice a day, by hand. My two older brothers and I did all the milking and feeding; I never figured out what my stepfather did while we worked. He always managed to slip off before the work began, not returning until dinner time.

By and by, we sold the farm and moved to a small rural town in the panhandle of Western Oklahoma. Despite its dwarf size, it was a damn site more entertaining than life on the farm. It didn't take long to befriend all the kids in our small school; we only had 150 students combined and that includes K1- 12. It was a nice little town, but somewhat boring after a while—the main attraction was to "drag" main every evening, all one mile of it. Like I said, sort of boring.

After my father went broke for the third time - he was a cattleman - he moved the family to Abilene, Texas. Now Abilene was a big town, at least to me. This was my first experience at feeling like I didn't fit in. There were two high schools and hundreds of students in each of them. I felt like a fish out of water and a bit homesick for school buddies I left behind, especially my red headed girlfriend. I dropped out of school my senior year and joined the Navy – I was off to see the world, least that's what the recruiter told me.

Over the next three years, I sailed the Mediterranean and visited nearly every port city on the north and east side of the sea—from Spain to Istanbul and everywhere in between. Now that was exciting. Among other things, I learned to drink, fight and haggle with the prostitutes. I definitely had a girlfriend in every port, at least a favorite hooker. It was so beautiful that I soon forgot about my many friends back home. There are no words to describe the exhilaration and elation one feels while sitting on the fantail of a large carrier in the middle of the night watching the moon, sea cows, whales, dolphins and an occasional cruise ship.

By the end of my tour, I was ready to go home, get married and try my hand at college. The University of Texas agreed to accept me, on a provisional basis, that is, providing I maintained a minimum of a "C" average. I married at the end of my third cruise, so my wife and I headed west out of Virginia to Austin, Texas. While registering at UT, I ran in to a stranger who told me about this wonderful small college on the south side of town—St. Edward's University. I can't explain why, but I dropped UT and entered St. Edward's. My senior year, my wife got pregnant and we moved to the panhandle of Texas to work for a cattle feed yard where my father was employed as a cattle buyer. The job provided health insurance, which we desperately needed. Within two months of arriving at my new job, an open silage pit caved in on me, breaking about every bone in my body, nearly suffocating me. While buried, I listened as my breathing slowly stopped--it was like watching my own death in slow motion. I wasn't scared. Actually, I felt quite snug; it was so comforting, warm and restful. During this twilight time, I saw this telescoping tunnel with a brilliant light at the other end and in that light stood a figure, a figure that looked like the Bible version of Christ. No words were exchanged but the communication flowed bilaterally for some time, or so it seemed. I finally relaxed, realizing death was imminent when an overwhelming feeling swept over me; I was in the company of something or someone very spiritual. It was at this point, I had an epiphany; I wasn't alone. I realized that humanity is but a microscopic cell, a part of a much larger body. We are all "worker bees", doing our part to keep the host parent well and alive.

Before I had recovered completely, my wife gave birth to our first born, a beautiful little dark haired boy. He died within three days of Hyaline Membrane disease, which forms a lining covering the lungs and results in death by suffocation. Just like my ordeal, except he didn't come back to life. When I finally got out of the hospital, my wife and I returned to Austin so I could complete my degree. I found work as an apartment manager, in a place I had worked at previously. Things got a little strange. For some inexplicable reason, I had this compulsion to sleep with every woman I met. I burned the candle at both ends up until graduation and on in to graduate school. When I became exhausted, I'd take amphetamines to revitalize my brain. Speed exacerbated my sexual appetite and my metabolism in general, so much so that I ran for Mayor in the early 70's. In retrospect, I see my behavior as an effort to amass "power" and fame.

One evening my father called me with a job offer in Aspen. I didn't even think about it, I accepted. Within ninety days of arriving in Aspen, I felt and acted, like a local; drinking all night and sleeping only when exhaustion dictated. Aspen was a very small community back then; there were only 1,700 hundred people who lived there year-round and that included the celebrities; such as John D., Jill St. John, Leon Uris and a few other starlets. It was like the Mediterranean on steroids. Booze, drugs, women everywhere, and all within a seven block square. A few years later, I sobered up to realize I was penniless, with no family—my wife left me and took the children with her. I returned to Texas.

Back in Dallas, I started life over again. Starting at the bottom of the food chain, I worked my way up from a tractor operator to a recruiter; I even completed my MBA. Only thing that didn't change was my behavior - I still loved wine, women and white-crosses. I made an attempt to settle down, I got married, then I got married again and again. Today I'm in my "Golden Years". Recently, the doctor told me: "You have a Bipolar Disorder, Type I. You've probably had it all your life." With this, I had another epiphany: "Now I get it, I understand my rather bizarre behavior over the years. But how did I get the disorder?" The enlightenment was about forty years too late, but then again one is never too old to begin anew.

Take a tour with a bipolar through Austin, Aspen and beyond. Feel the fun as well as the insanity, pain and frustration, and view the fanciful aberrations I awoke to each morning, for forty years.

Introduction

My story is of a child who grew up with stunning successes, one after another. After a near-death experience in the late 60s however, family and friends saw changes in my personality — some immediately, some over the course of time. Me? The only change I noticed was my ability to foresee events before they occurred.

Bipolarity is not something people expect, especially if you've been a "good" kid. Okie born and Okie reared on a small dirt farm in the mouth of the Panhandle, I learned to appreciate what I had rather than what I wanted. Needs were simple. There was a parlor pot in each bedroom and an outhouse in the back. Sears Roebuck supplied wiping paper as well as entertainment . . . an outhouse just wouldn't be complete without a copy of a catalogue filled with glossy pictures of women's underwear. Life on the farm was simple and uncomplicated, never boring. Polio was the talk of the times, hitting nearly one family in each of the surrounding communities. Manic depression was unheard of, let alone bipolar disorder.

Alcohol was available through moonshiners and bootleggers but was not widely used. The strongest chemical we kept around the farm was DDT. We weren't concerned about it at the time. Either use it or lose a crop, maybe some cattle. Vegetables and grains were 100% organic, fertilized with the best chicken shit in the land.

How could one grow up in this Utopian setting and later morph into a bipolar maniac? The transformation is so subtle, so gradual that one never suspects the storm looming over the horizon. Like the cicada, it can remain dormant for years then, one day, all hell breaks loose.

I've tried to come to grips with my bizarre life. What triggered the transformation? Was it the DDT? Some say perhaps the hardships of growing up poor had something to do with it. I say not. Then again, I ingested many a vial of amphetamines in undergraduate school. Was that the trigger? Was it my near-death experience? There is no doubt an NDE can — and will — radically alter one's perception of life. It changes the perception of what is right and what is wrong; what is important and what is bullshit.

Aimed at the American Dream

Like many a boy who grew up in the Oklahoma Panhandle, I left high school my senior year to join the Navy and see some of the world. I had the usual adventures and learning experiences and met my soon-to-be wife. In January, 1966 I finished my hitch and said goodbye to the Naval Air Station at Oceana, VA. I was twenty-one, married, full of piss and vinegar and grandiose plans to attend college. I had earned my GED and got to take a few college level courses while aboard the aircraft carrier USS Saratoga. The University of Texas in Austin accepted my application for enrollment on a provisional basis — provisional because I had not completed high school.

Kari Ann, my new wife, and I purchased a red Reliant convertible prior to my discharge. With separation papers in hand and a little over $200 between us we headed west out of Oceana, bound for Austin, Texas. Neither of us knew with any degree of certainty what we were really going to do when we got there, but we were going nonetheless. It was as though a "tractor beam" was tugging us. We arrived in the Smokies with just enough daylight left to see the rustic cabins, clinging precariously to the side of the mountains. Pots, pans, washbasins — you name it — hung in front of the little shanties. Although we didn't see any, I am sure there were white lightning stills in the back. We drove along the river by night. The full moon glistened off the surface, tempting us to stop and admire. If we had not been in such a hurry to get to Austin, we would have obliged but we had to keep going. We had no time to stop and smell the roses. We barely had enough money for gas and food, let alone souvenir shops and lodging. To make things worse, we were ticketed in Georgia for speeding — four miles outside of town. A small-town speed trap. Welcome home, sailor. You are now back in America. Your money is ours. And don't forget to have a good day." At least, that's what I thought the officer said.

Onward we went, switching driving duties as needed. I am not sure if either of us slept during the entire thirty hour trip. It we got any sleep at all, it was just in fits and starts, never sinking into the delta stage of deep rest.

Late in the evening of the second day, we arrived in Austin, too pooped to think and too weak from hunger to walk. Kari suggested we stop so she could take a pee and call her parents. They were thrilled to hear we had arrived and came to guide us in. I guess they thought we were much too addled to find their house on our own. At that point, they were probably correct.

Arrival in Austin

Spring semester was already underway at the University of Texas, so we wasted no time looking for work. Within a week, Kari landed a coveted state job. Getting a job with the state was like getting a tenured position at the university — you were safe. I found my own job about two weeks later with Westinghouse, installing wiring for the new "direct dial" telephone conversion. Our combined income exceeded our expectations, as well as our requirements. Sweet, for a couple who only a few weeks before had nothing. But I found myself at a crossroads. "Do I continue to work for the rest of my life, or do I start college?"

College won out. I was to become just another full-time student. The GI stipend at that time was $50 per month — just enough to put beans, rice, bread and bologna on the table. I was exhilarated, happy and very frustrated. Here I have this great job, making more money than I ever thought possible, and now I have to quit to become a poor college student?

"How am I going to pay the $12 per semester hour and still have money for books? How am I to get to school? Kari has to have transportation to her job — she's the chief wage earner. I have no idea how all this is going turn out — seems improbable. Oh well, these things will work themselves out," I thought. And so went the voices of the committee inside my head. In reality, only a fool would take up the challenge. For some insane reason I just felt "special" - a cut above others.

Snap Decision

Summer semester was to begin on Monday. The only thing remaining was to stand in line and pay my tuition fee. Lines at UT were unbelievably long. There were close to 350 students inside the administration building and another 500 or so lined up two blocks down the street. Two dozen clerks processed students' registration and collected their money. Classes filled rapidly. It was a first-come, first-served basis. If one absolutely had to have a particular class, he or she nearly had to camp there overnight. I still had to shop for books. Most UT students purchased their books at the Co-Op. The Co-Op had been selling books to UT students since 1896, about as long as the university had been a college. The store was, and still is, a legend. It's a two story building on Guadalupe Street, directly across from the campus. The bottom floor is filled with row after row of books — both used and new. The smell of mildew is so thick you can cut it with a knife. The top floor is mostly paraphernalia — UT jerseys, caps, blankets and the usual things with mascot symbols sewn on them. While shopping for used textbooks at the Co-Op, I met Jim Siptak for the first time. We swapped stories for a bit.

"I'm enrolled at St. Edward's Catholic University" he said.

"Where is that?"

"South of here, near I-35."

"Why are you going there? Why not UT?" I asked.

"The classes are smaller at St. Ed's — you get more help from the teachers."

"What's it cost?"

"It's expensive — about $250 per semester hour, per course."

"How in the shit can you afford that?"

"My folks pay for it."

"Are they rich?" I asked.

"I wouldn't say rich. My dad is a country doctor in Dime Box. So was Granddad. Why don't you see if you can get in out there?"

"I can't afford it. Besides, classes start here at UT Monday."

"I'm sure you can get a student loan from St. Edward's. They're very generous about that."

"Shit, I'm confused enough. It took everything we have just for me to be standing here now. Don't screw with my mind!" I laughed.

"Ah, come on. I'll take you out there right now. If you're not accepted, you still have time to shop for books. You'll see. We'll go to the Student Affairs office and see if they'll loan you the money first."

Filled with apprehension, I agreed to go with Jim. I liked this guy from the get-go. He was six feet tall, a bit over 160 pounds, premature receding hairline and about as sincere a fellow as I had ever met. He was very different from the sailors I had lived with for the past three years. His language was refined, not what I was accustomed to hearing. For one thing, he didn't cuss.

We dropped our book shopping, got in his Olds and off we went. St. Edward's was a twenty-minute drive from UT. When we arrived, I was shocked. St. Edward's was just a small campus. St. Ed's and UT were built within two years of one another, and the UT campus covered 350 acres and had some 350 buildings — some new, some old. St. Edward's, on the other hand, sat on about forty acres, and had twenty-five buildings, only one of which was new. The new building housed the classrooms. The campus was quaint, but comfortable. Dormitories for the Holy Cross brothers and students, administrative offices, bookstore, and chapel occupied the older buildings. UT was oil rich, mostly from endowments; St. Edward's was dirt poor and relied heavily on donations.

We walked up the flight of cobblestone steps into one of the oldest limestone buildings, probably circa 1885. A musty smell permeated the air. There was no central air, just window units. Jim led me to the Student Affairs office. We went inside, but I was scared shitless. I could hardly think, let alone speak, but he did the talking. Within three minutes, they pretty much knew my full story.

Unbelievably, they accepted me on the spot. The administrative clerk informed me I would have to complete the paperwork that day if I was to get in the summer classes. I reiterated that I only made $50 a month from the VA and had no other means of income.

"We can get you approved for a student loan if you're serious about attending classes here."

He processed my loan and another clerk accepted me into the school. A third person enrolled me in a speech class — about the only class remaining open at that late date. All this in less than two hours. It was a far cry from the long lines at UT. For the first time since arriving in Austin, I was sure I was going to get an education. My smile must have been as wide as the keyboard on a grand piano.

Jim took me back to the bookstore where we first met. I bid him farewell and walked back to my apartment. To this day, I believe that the meeting with Jim at the Co-Op was divinely inspired.

Selling the Plan

I had no idea what my wife would think about this humongous debt we were about to incur. Kari was not only my spouse; she was my lover and best friend.

I paced the floor in the little bungalow, anxiously awaiting her return. "What the hell am I going to tell her? Even worse, what the hell is she going to say?"

About 5:30, Kari arrived home from work. I could hear her walking up the rickety flight of wooden stairs. I thought I would piss my pants, my heart was pounding so madly. In she came and gave me a cheerful hug and a peck on the cheek. She told me all about her day. Then the inevitable happened.

"How did you do today? Were you able to get all your books? Did you have enough cash?"

"Sit down," I said. "There has been a change of plans."

I could see by the look on her face that she was expecting me to say that I had changed my mind about attending college. God knows, I barely had the courage to tell her all that had happened. I told her all about my shopping spree and meeting Jim. This relieved her somewhat. I grimaced, and then told her about changing colleges from a cheap one that we could afford in favor of one that cost about $1800 per semester.

She took it all in stride and, like me, believed it would all work out. Talk about two kids with an abundance of faith; that was us. Full steam ahead and hang the future — that was our motto.

We worked out the logistic issues. I would take her to work and pick her up when she got off. By the time the summer course was over, we had two cars. I purchased an old '55 Ford that looked like shit but ran okay. I had to install signal lights and seat belts but, other than that, it served me well.

Into a War Zone

The only class remaining open at that late date at St. Edward's was speech. I didn't even know what speech was. I thought it had something to do with foreign languages. The professor was a retired thespian director, with a list of accomplishments to his credit as long as a country mile. He had fantastic people skills and sympathetically reminded me of my use of double negatives. I worked my ass off trying to master the class.

By the time the semester was over, I had made an "A." My confidence was ten-fold compared to what it was when I first set foot in the classroom. More importantly, I made friends with fellow students — some of whom I still maintain contact with forty years after our initial meeting.

Steve Polvent was one such classmate who became a friend. Steve was from Queens, NY. His father worked two jobs so Steve could attend St. Edwards. Steve was married and had two beautiful little girls with whom he lived with in South Lamar, about five miles from the campus.

At the end of the course, each student had to give a speech in front of the rest of the class. My speech covered the high prices of pharmaceutical products. Informative, but not very moving. Steve's speech was about the undeclared war in Vietnam. He had served as an Air Force photographer, stationed near Saigon. It included some very graphic pictures of children kicking the detached head of a Viet Cong soldier as if it was a soccer ball on the playground. I learned about presenting a topic with intensity from Steve.

Summer school was over. After finals, Steve, Jim and I went to Schultz's Beer Garden on San Jacinto — a stone's throw from the UT campus. We had just started our third beer when a man wearing carpenter coveralls came running in screaming, "The Tower is on fire. Looks like the fire is at the top."

The Tower, a landmark limestone building at the center of the UT campus, stands 307 feet tall. It's visible from nearly anywhere in Austin.

That was all the reason we needed to finish our beer and rush to the Campus. Badass mistake. The first thing we saw was a young man who looked to be about twenty kneeling in the middle of an intersection shooting towards the Tower. He was dressed in bib coveralls and his hair was long, almost touching his shoulders. He had a bolt-action rifle cradled on his knee. He must have been an undercover officer.

"What the hell? He's firing at the Tower," I shouted.

Bullets ripped into the Tower's limestone walls, throwing out enough dust to be confused with smoke from a fire.

I thought a revolution had broken out. We looked at each other as if one of us should know the answer. A police officer rushed up to us screaming, "There's a shooter on the Tower! Take cover!"

The sound of sirens resonated through the air. Ambulances and police cars lined Guadalupe Street, just west of the campus. The area looked like a movie set, with bodies everywhere. I remember two paramedics picking up one student to put him on the stretcher. It looked like he'd lost his left arm. Bullets were riddling the vehicles. Rescuers were putting their own lives at risk.

"We should go to the hospital to offer blood. They're going to need a lot of it," Steve said.

When we got there, we saw ambulances lining the entrance to the emergency room, some carrying two victims, others just one. Everyone, including citizens, assisted in unloading them. People were bewildered, moving about without knowing what was happening.

The shooter turned out to be Charles Whitman — a promising graduate student studying architectural engineering. I suspect he was high on amphetamines and deprived of sleep — like many students I knew. He was an ex-Marine, living on the GI Bill. He worked at the Health Clinic. He had a wife and mother, both of whom lived and worked in Austin. He had murdered the two of them the night before. At the end of his shooting spree, sixteen people lay dead, and thirty-two wounded.

The Tower had a history of tragedy. In 1974, the daughter of the Dean of Business, high on LSD, performed a swan dive from the top of the tower. After Whitman's rampage and several suicides from it, the university closed the observation deck. In 1999, it was reopened after the installation of a steel barricade around the top.

Juggling Monks and Bunks

I carried twelve semester hours my first regular semester. Carrying a full load was a tough transition for me, but I was mostly holding my own. However, I was having problems with my English professor, Brother Charles Anderson — a monk and a tough old bird. I thought maybe he didn't like ex-military students.

Steve said, "Take him a bottle of scotch. He likes scotch." I thought he was joking.

"Damn! That's bribery."

"That is the way it works," Steve assured me.

He made an appointment to see Brother Charles. We visited him about six p.m. in his eight foot by twelve foot residence. He invited us in and Steve said, "Ray has a gift for you." I handed him the bottle of Vat 69. It seems the Brother couldn't have cared less about my military service. He thanked me and bid us farewell.

I shook my head as I walked back to the car. "I can't believe I just did that."

Much to my chagrin, it didn't make a damned bit of difference. If anything, Brother Charles was even tougher on me than before. I buckled down and made it through, though.

I was not so direct with my other professors. Instead of outright bribery, Kari, Steve and I hosted a party at Steve's apartment complex and invited all the professors, and a few influential students. That did have an impact. And no, we didn't invite Brother Charles. Sailing was smooth from then on. Both my wife and I learned to love the Brothers. They became confidantes, friends, companions and fellow chefs.

Time flew during the first year. Then Kari and I fell into another gift from the Almighty. We purchased a home in what is now a desirable neighborhood for $1.00 down with my VA benefits. The furnishings came with the home. Hell, we were now "upper class." We moved into the house. As we sunk deeper into debt, I had to find an additional job. My wife was working full-time for the State

Education Department, and attending a class during her lunch hour at the University of Texas. Finally, I found an attendant's job on the graveyard shift at the Austin State School for mentally handicapped children. It was a good fit for my schedule — the majority of the children on my ward were well-behaved and slept most of the night, leaving me plenty of time to study.

There was no money to do anything but some meager groceries and pay utilities. I knew of people in East Austin (the poorest community in Austin at the time) who ate better than we did, but then again, neither of us like the taste of opossum or raccoon. It finally struck me that we couldn't afford our $87 house payment.

I landed a job as an apartment manager. The job included the benefit of a furnished free apartment, but no pay. With my class schedule, night job and my responsibilities as manager, I could barely stay awake in class. One nun kicked me out of her class (Russian history) for sleeping. It was an 8:00 a.m. class. She was much worse than Brother Charles. She had no tolerance for students who had to work. I was forced to give up my night job at the State School.

Sleep deprivation and poor study habits hounded me. A neighbor of ours - a doctoral candidate in Philosophy - told me about a wonder drug.

"It's food for the brain," he said.

He made a damn good spokesperson for the drug's manufacturer. Thus began a long love affair. My neighbor was right. Amphetamines were indeed "food for the brain." Nearly any family doctor would write a prescription for Dexedrine - the brand name for the drug. Students lived on them. Housewives used it as a diet pill. Police officers popped them like candy. One officer told me it kept him alert. Can you imagine an entire police department high on speed?

It sure worked for me but continued use wreaked havoc on my personality. The highs were great; the lows were hell. I couldn't sleep. I tried wine, then beer but nothing seemed to slow my mind enough for me to sleep. It's amazing what the human body can become accustomed to, but there's always a cost . . . and it usually gets paid later. My payback was a fried brain, which might well explain the nightmare that lay before me.

I became more reliant on amphetamines. To hell with sleep.

Sleep deprivation and excessive doses of amphetamines were slowly driving me insane. I became a bit of a recluse and developed other antisocial abnormalities, the most dangerous being anger.

Feeling the Strain

Everything changed in January of '67. St. Ed's went co-ed. There was a sudden influx of young, attractive women on campus. All the horny young men, including myself, went a bit crazy. Many of the females had gone to all-girls Catholic schools their entire K-12 years and they were just as horny as the boys were. Things changed that semester, for the worse as far as studying.

I can't tell you how much frustration and chaos that created for the nuns of the school. Yeah, the nuns came along when we made the transfer from all-male to co-ed. After all, who else was going to keep the girls in check? The boys were like all young men — walking around in clouds of testosterone. Hard dicks everywhere. The girls were as horny as dogs in heat, with just a handful of nuns to police their sexual appetites. Perhaps the girls were simply revolting against their past cloistered life. As skirts got shorter, concentration went to hell.

Spring semester was underway. The Brothers may have seemed mean-spirited taskmasters, but they were masters when it came to education. Stretched to my max, broke, and confused, I was competing against kids three years my junior who had more and better education. I felt overwhelmed.

Leaning on Crank

Kari and I were the poorest of the poor. Strapped for cash, we improvised our own entertainment. Some weekends my friends from school gathered for barbecue country ribs, corn on the cob and chicken necks. For the most part we just shared the cheapest of beer, covered dishes of pastas, bean salads and cheese sandwiches. The fact that we were all poor helped — being broke carried no stigma among us.

The men got together frequently just to break the tedium of studying. Such meetings revolved around activities that were cost-free, or at least inexpensive, such as fishing on the local lakes, or on the Pedernales River. One night we were on the river (downstream from Willie Nelson's house) drinking Black Label beer, pretending to be "fishing". It was two or three in the morning and we were shitfaced. Steve - my friend from Queens - yelled out, "Look at that! The bass are hitting the chicken necks!"

I don't know why, but we laughed our asses off, hooting and hollering as if we were stoned. Campers along the river began shining their spotlights on us — this did tend to dampen our party. We decided Steve was full of shit (and cheap beer).

The more speed I consumed, the more delusional I became. At times, I would have to stick my finger into an image (or a person) to verify if it (or he/she) was real. I embarrassed myself more than once. One morning, after a sleepless night, I slipped two bottles of Mad Dog 20/20 into the saddlebags of my old worn-out Suzuki motorcycle. The bike was intended to get me back and forth to school, a six-mile round trip ride but I wanted to ride it to Bastrop State Park, about ten miles beyond Bergstrom Air Force Base. I wasn't quite sure it would make the trip but I took off anyway. I didn't have a reason to go to the park — just another compulsion.

Buried Alive

My third year in college Kari was pregnant with our first child. Now, we really were in deep shit. We had no insurance and no money. I called my father and asked if he could find me a job that provided insurance.

"Sure. Come to work for the yard," he said. He was a buyer for a large commercial cattle feed yard.

It was late fall. The morning air was quite brisk and getting cooler by the day. Soon winter would be upon us. Kari was due to give birth in March. I dropped my classes, borrowed $500 from the American Bank, and off we went to Perryton, Texas. The feed yard assigned me to the feed mill. The mill blended fodder (silage) with rolled grains such as corn and oats. It was instrumental in keeping the feed yard profitable. Feed-yard cattle are fed three times a day, and the yards make their money selling feed to the people who own the cattle.

It was now January 1969. My father asked me to go down into the fodder silo — an open trench about the width of three Greyhound buses, 200 yards long and thirty feet deep. Insurance auditors were coming the next day to review operations. Their findings determined the worker compensation insurance rate for the next 12 months. The loader arm was not long enough to reach the top of the pit, forcing the operators to dig out the center, allowing gravity to bring down the top layer. The pit had a history of caving in and crushing the loading equipment.

Winter in the plains area of the Panhandle was brutal. No trees — only tumbleweeds. Despite the 20 degree temperature, the sun was bright and the wind calm. I was wearing long handle thermal underwear and three layers of clothes on top, topped off with a heavy goose down coat. Of course, I had to wear my "cowboy" hat. It just wouldn't look right to go without it, not in the midst of the "real" cowboys who worked there.

I drove my pickup truck down inside the pit, parking about thirty feet from the edge. Sitting between my pickup and the pit was a tractor with a loader attached to the front, and a two-ton Chevy truck. It didn't take long to see the problem. The center of the pit was so spooned out it looked like an entrance to a cave. I just stood there pondering what I should do to straighten out the mess before the insurance boys showed up. It was obvious that in the future we would have to use equipment with a longer reach, or dig from the top of the pit.

While evaluating the situation, a clump of the compressed fodder weighing several tons caved in from the top. I never heard a sound. There was total silence. I was buried two feet below the surface. The up-thrust from the mass of saturated fodder blew the hood off the truck. I realized I was trapped in the fodder and grain. Initially, I struggled to free myself. I pulled so hard that I popped the joints in four of the fingers on my right hand. It was hopeless, my limbs were essentially paralyzed, but there was no pain.

One of the warmest, most soothing feelings of serenity blanketed me. A tunnel gradually began forming, sort of like a telescoping funnel. The tunnel reminded me of a tin horn. At the far end was this terrifically brilliant and inviting light. The light was not blinding — it was more like a soothing light from a warm fireplace. In the center of the tunnel, the figure of a man began materializing. The figure then came into focus. It was an image of Christ — white robe, long dark hair and a beard, his hands to his sides. I felt no fearful emotions whatsoever. No spoken words, but perfect communication. This figure, bathed in the most radiant light I had ever seen, stood motionless. It was perfect peace. There were no relatives to greet me. No friends. No demons. I felt so snug. There was no pain. No panic. Just an extremely blissful state of comfort. The setting was warm, inviting, and I wanted to stay there forever. Death never entered my mind. To this day, I yearn to experience this state of being again.

Some medical "professionals" claim the "tunnel of light" is a hallucination, triggered by the brain shutting down from oxygen deprivation. Neither I nor they can prove or disprove this thesis. I can tell you that the return to life is realistic to those of us who have experienced this sensation.

Jim, the mill manager, happened to be near the pit at the time of the cave in. He might even have been the one who caused the pit to cave in by driving on top of the silo. I snapped out of my stupor. There was something standing on top of me. I could feel the added pressure. Or was there? "Go away," I said to myself. "Leave me alone."

My father told me later that it was Jim who called the office on his two-way radio. Jim told him: "The pit caved in on Ray. Get some cowboys down here. Bring pitchforks and shovels. I need help."

Both my pregnant wife and father worked in the administrative offices, about a quarter mile from the pits. When my father heard the news, he warned the others not to tell my wife until he had a chance to see me.

It seemed to be hours later when I opened my eyes to see the cowboys using pitchforks, shovels and their hands to dig. One of the men fainted. Others were pale as a ghost. I saw my father kneeling at my side. He was weeping. I couldn't understand what they were doing, or why. I was on my back, but couldn't see both legs. There was no pain. So why were they all around me?

My right leg and left arm were paralyzed. I couldn't move either. I was not breathing, nor did I want to. I was at peace. I found out later why my arm and leg wouldn't move — both had compound fractures. My father told me it was a grisly scene; thigh bones were protruding through the skin in several places and the humerus bone poked through my left arm. Both the arm and leg were twisted upside down; they crossed each other behind my head.

My Stetson probably saved my life by covering my face. It had captured just enough air to supply my lungs while the men dug me out.

The ambulance arrived with two flat tires. The company veterinary surgeon sent for his station wagon. The ghostly gray cowboys finished digging me out. One told me later that I was limp as a wet dish cloth when they stuffed my body into the back of the station wagon. I could tell my father was in the driver's seat, but who was this man in the back with me? Then I remembered: the vet. I heard him say to my dad, "I'm going to have to perform a tracheotomy on him. He's not breathing."

The thought of him cutting a hole into my neck with the same pocketknife he had just used to castrate fifty calves was enough to stimulate my breathing. I asked the vet to roll down the window a bit so I could get some cool air. I could hear the two of them breathe a sigh of relief. From the moment I took my first breath the pain began.

Near Death's Door

The feed yard was about twenty-five miles from the nearest hospital. By the time we got there, the emergency room staff was assembled and waiting to treat me for shock. I remember two nurses cutting through my three layers of clothing.

"My hand is cramping. Someone help me!" yelled one of the nurses.

"Here, cut his boots off while I finish his clothes," directed the second. It seemed like they cut clothes from my body for twenty or thirty minutes.

"Put a compression pack on his femoral artery. His femur is sticking out. It could puncture the artery," the first said. I could hear everything, but then I blacked out. When I awoke, I was in the back of another station wagon — a real ambulance. The siren was blaring out a cacophonous, irritating noise, keeping me from slipping back into my state of tranquility. "Where am I? Where are we going?" I asked.

There was no response. I was covered with sheets and a blanket — perhaps to keep me warm, but more likely to keep me from seeing my body. "His leg and arm bones are visible," the ambulance driver told my dad. It was probably a good thing I couldn't see.

Three months and multiple surgeries later, they fitted my leg with a brace. Paralyzed, the left arm was fitted with its own contraption. I had so much metal in my body I could- and did - set off metal detectors. I learned to walk on my new brace. It took me a while, but I learned. One day, while at the feed yard thanking everyone for their help, I walked by the vet's office — the same man who accompanied me to the emergency room. Doc said to me:

"Ray, walk by my office again." I did as he requested.

"You have a loose screw. It happens sometimes with cattle after we install metal splints for broken legs. The screws tend to work loose."

The company had a plane and a darn good pilot. The pilot flew me to Oklahoma City to have adjustments made to my walking brace. On our flight back to Perryton, we stopped by the hospital in Shattuck, Oklahoma, where the orthopedic surgeon who had pieced me back together practiced. Doc insisted on x-rays. When he saw the results, he turned to the pilot and said, "You are going home alone. His leg broke again, breaking the metal plate in half." The plate was the only thing holding my femur together.

"Here we go again," I thought to myself. "Another surgery." I woke up during this one. I watched the gruesome operation as Doctor Burgtorff removed the broken piece of metal. He used a saw, a hammer and an electric drill. The skin and muscle tissue were pulled out of the way of the metal plate and held open with what appeared to be four "C" clamps. I saw the procedure in total — perfectly. I know I did. But the operating room staff said I didn't wake up.

"You must have been dreaming."

"I was not dreaming. I can tell you everything you did. I also recall screaming for morphine while in recovery."

The nurses were not at all convinced. Nevertheless, it was true.

And so ended my first life. With death behind me, I entered a new era.

A Life Too Short

Three months later, while I was still recovering in the hospital, my first child was born. Our tiny boy was so precious in every way. He had dark hair, like me, and long eyebrows. His little fingers, although quite thin even for a baby, were long. After two days, the hospital staff told Kari and me that James Bradley wouldn't live. He died the next day.

I was devastated. Kari walked around with a blank look on her face. They took me to the graveside funeral in an ambulance, most likely the same one they had used to transport me from one hospital to the other after my accident.

With tears running down my face, I watched as they lowered James into his own earthen pit. I had nearly died from suffocation and a mixture of methane gas. James died from hyaline membrane disease, suffocation from a coating inside his lungs. I can only hope his trip to the other side was as euphoric as my own.

After "Death"

Many who have had a near-death experience report a significant change in their behavior, belief system, self-esteem, and spirituality. Likewise, I experienced many of those changes, but my reaction to them was somehow different. Like the majority, I also got a divorce, then another, and another and then one more. After the fourth divorce, I realized the problem was me, not my wives. Unlike some of the others who have had an NDE, I never became complacent, smug in the knowledge that I now understood the "true meaning of life".

There is some scientific evidence that the right temporal lobe of the brain houses an area called the "God" area. When stimulated, test subjects reported experiencing some of the same emotions NDE'rs reported, such as a sense of well-being, the presence of others about them, and a desire to return. (For example, see The Discovery Channel's program "Morgan Freeman: Through the Wormhole".)

"A ...NDE not only changes an individual's life, but often radically transforms it," says Dr. Kenneth Ring in his book *Heading Toward Omega*. Although I didn't notice an immediate change in my behavior, many friends and relatives did. No one pointed out this change. I guess they were trying to be courteous or - more likely - they didn't want to suffer the wrath of my retaliatory response. Years later, at my daughter's wedding in Austin, my first wife's parents brought up the subject. They both said the change was sudden, shocking. My personality had changed 180 degrees from life before death. I knew I had become a bit of a menace to society. What I didn't know was that others saw it too.

At home, I perceived myself as a kind and considerate husband, but my close friends and associates knew the other side of my personality. The once loyal and trustworthy husband, casual dresser, mild mannered, monogamist, low-key homebody was now a sexual predator, heavy drinker, boisterous, argumentative, confrontational, lavish dresser, with an exaggerated sense of confidence. Prior to my NDE I was extremely cautious about spending money, what I said, and what I did. I quickly sidestepped anything resembling risk. Now risk-taking is my calling card. I thrive on risky relationships, sex, and investments; I need to face death to feel alive, or to feel anything, actually.

Apartment Romeo

With so much behind us, we returned to Austin that summer so I could finish my degree. I was still crippled from the accident, but I worked harder than ever. It was now my senior year. I had to graduate soon, or starve. We were able to get our previous jobs back — Kari as a state worker, me as an apartment manager. I called the owners of the complex I had worked for previously to inquire about finding another manager's job. They told me, "Just in time. The current managers are leaving next month. If you want the job, it's yours." I loved the couple who owned the apartments. They were kind, considerate and loved to drink Southern Comfort.

I met with the outgoing manager to transfer keys, codes, and to get the scoop on each of the tenants. From the moment I walked into the meeting, she was flirty. At one point, she brought me a cup of tea. I was sitting on a low sofa, which forced her to bend down a bit to hand the cup to me. She took the opportunity to make a bow, not a bend. She was bra-less and her breasts hung down, nearly popping out of her blouse. She looked at me to see if I was watching. I was staring all right, but I didn't make a pass. I thought it might have been a "test."

Several months after assuming responsibilities as manager, she dropped in to visit me. She "tested" me again. This time I felt obliged to have sex with her. "Damn, this job is wonderful," I said to myself.

Chateau Paris had 24 rental units, somewhat small for an apartment complex. I was hired to manage and maintain the grounds and apartments. I was fortunate to have the job. Married students stood in line for this type of position. The personalities and occupations of the tenants varied widely. We had two professors from UT, a well-to-do student from Florida, a political analyst, a banker, a few business people, a sprinkling of retired women, and a brilliant filmmaker, Tobe Hooper.

Tobe had a young son and an indiscreet wife, Frances. He spent a lot of time on the road. Although Tobe was extremely talented, his public persona was at odds with his private one. The public saw Tobe as a quiet, reflective genius. His wife told me about a darker side. She said he had a volatile temper. I don't know which of the two was the more violent, but I do know that a month didn't go by that I didn't receive a call from one of their neighbors demanding I tell Tobe and his wife to keep the noise down. They'd get into an argument and throw things around a bit. Sometimes one or both would get a bruise or two. I don't know what caused the injuries, but I had my suspicions. Frances was bigger than Tobe, both in height and weight, but she generally came out on the short end of the stick. Tobe's trademark was his cigarette-type cigars; Frances's sunglasses were hers. They didn't hide much. I asked her one time how she got the black eye. She told me her son swung open a door and hit her in the face. It sounded plausible, but I didn't believe her.

Frances called one morning to come get a turtle out of her disposal. It seems her young son had thrown the pet turtle in the sink. The turtle climbed down inside the disposal. While working at the sink, she came up behind me and flung her arms around me.

"I have wanted to do this from the first time I saw you without a shirt," she said. "Do you have time to fuck?"

Her bluntness left me speechless, but that didn't stop us from dashing to the bedroom. We locked the door behind us, stripped naked, and fell to the bed, wrapping our legs around each other like a couple of snakes in a mating ritual. Sex didn't last three hours. It was more like thirty minutes, which was thirty minutes more than I had intended. She was neither a "good" nor a "bad" lay, just another one. I never fell for her calls again. Once was enough. Tobe came in for the weekend and beat the shit out of her. Since Tobe wasn't bruised, I assume she didn't get in a punch.

Typically, I studied at night. A little speed and a pot of coffee kept me wired for five or six hours. About two in the morning, I heard a knock. I assumed it was a tenant wanting me to unlock their door — misplacing keys was a very common occurrence. I looked out the peep-hole. It was Tobe. I opened the door, expecting him to punch me right in the face.

"Ray, can I come in?" he said.

"Oh shit, Frances has told him about our fling," I thought.

"I saw your light on and thought I'd join you for a cup of coffee. Got any brewed?"

I always had coffee at the ready. Coffee and speed are like strawberries and cream, you can't have one without the other. Tobe was smoking one of his trademark cigars. I poured him a steaming cup of Cajun chicory coffee with a dab of whole cream poured on top.

"Someone stole all my camera equipment in Dallas yesterday. I stopped at a motel late in the night and decided it was safe to leave my gear in my car."

Tobe drove a small blue MG with a black ragtop. It wouldn't have taken much to break into.

"They got my best camera. I just bought that one, paid $2,500. Oh well, it was my fault. I shouldn't have left it in the car."

My mind raced wildly like a runaway locomotive. "I wonder if it was the camera he used to shoot the pastoral film he made for PBS. Is he here to quiz me about Frances? What's his motive? He's never stopped in before." My hands trembled, which was not that unusual for me.

After thirty minutes of trivial conversation, he said, "Got to go. See you around."

Did he know, or did he not know? I couldn't sleep the rest of the night. At this point, adultery might as well have been murder — I couldn't have felt more guilty.

Later, I bumped into Tobe at a client's office in Austin. He was there to see the same person I had come to see. We acknowledged each other, but didn't strike up a conversation. I was as nervous as a whore in church. That was the last time I saw Tobe.

Tobe and Frances divorced. He went on to produce lots of wildly popular full-length movies: The Texas Chainsaw Massacre, Salem's Lot, Poltergeist,

Freddy's Nightmares, Tales from the Crypt, and various others.

During this summer of unbridled wildness, a young black girl strolled through our courtyard. "She's probably casing the place," I thought. "Or is she here to steal money from the coke machine or the laundry?"

I confronted her. "What are you doing?"

"Looking for work," she replied.

"What kind of work?"

"Anything. I'm a single mom and need some work," she said.

"I'll see what I can find. Is your baby a boy or girl?"

"He's a little boy."

"How old?" I asked.

"He's three months."

She was damn fine looking. Built like a model, with huge hooters, slim waist, and doe-like brown eyes. My mind switched to sex. She wanted work, and I wanted her. "I've got to find something for her to do," I thought. I wanted her to stick around. "Who knows, she might even repay me with a piece of ass."

I found some menial work for her, cleaning vacant apartments. She later began cleaning tenants' apartments. She had five or six clients — just enough to keep her coming back.

One day, she came up to me.

"Is there anything else I can do today? I'm through cleaning."

"Well, there is something. You could have sex with me. I don't have much money. Maybe three dollars."

She nodded her consent.

"Go to number 15. Here's the key."

I took the long way around, out of sight from the other residents. I walked into the apartment to find her petite little butt on the bed, as if to say, "What took you so long?" I ripped my clothes off, flinging them to the floor.

"You white guys are not afraid of taking your clothes off in front of a girl."

"Are you going to have sex with yours on?" I asked.

Nervously, she slowly removed all her clothes. I don't ever recall being as aroused. I remember thinking, "Damn, she looks delicious."

I hopped on before she could change her mind. She was an awesome lay. Her vagina was tight for a mother of a three-month-old. Her vulva reminded me of a camel-toe, but not as exaggerated. I poked her with everything I had, wishing I had another six inches. No doubt, I could have definitely made love to her for three hours — but not that day. I knew Kari would be home soon. Moreover, there was no one in the office to answer the phone. I gave her three dollars in quarters. We both left happy.

Over the next few weeks, we made love when and where possible. She was as good in bed the second and third time as she was the first.

But I'd given her power over me. She could now go tell my wife about our fun and games if I tried to reprimand or correct her in any way. Her confidence grew. One day I noticed some of my quarters from the coke machine were missing. I had the quarters laid out on my desk waiting to account for them. I suspected her, but didn't say anything.

Blackmailed

Later that week, one of the tenants, Susanne, came to see me and said, "Ray, someone stole a check from our apartment and forged my signature. It was only ten dollars, but if they'll steal $10, they'll eventually steal $100."

I thought she was accusing me.

"Damn, it wasn't me. I haven't been inside your apartment."

"No. We didn't think you had anything to do with it, but we do suspect Rose." She cleaned their apartment weekly. "Oh shit! What do you want me to do?"

"I don't know what you can do, other than to get her out of here."

"Please call your bank, Susanne. See if they will get your money back."

"Okay. I'll do that." She called the bank — they refunded her $10.

Rosie had me by the gonads and she knew it. At first she took money from the vending machines, then she overcharged her clients, and finally she got brazen enough to forge a check taken from one her client's checkbook.

I had no choice. I had to report her forgery even if she told my wife and the entire city of Austin of our tryst. I called the police department to ask them if there was anything I should do, such as file a charge against her.

"What's her name?" the officer asked.

"Rose Williams."

There was a moment of ominous silence. "She has a history of stealing and forging, and she's only seventeen."

I learned a valuable lesson. Never ever sleep with an employee.

No sooner had that fling ended than a tenant's sixteen-year-old daughter began coming to my office during the day when Kari was at work. Kathleen was about the most over-developed teenager I'd ever seen. She wore a tiny bikini during the day — probably even slept in it. I knew better than to have sex with her. She would no doubt get pregnant. She was too young to get birth control pills — her mother would have had a hissy if she knew she even wanted them. I didn't use condoms, so she was safe.

Later that summer, one of our male tenants came to me in a rage. He was a strikingly handsome man of thirty-something, married, and the father of an eight-year-old girl. He was pissed.

"Ray! Kathleen groped me while I was swimming with my daughter. It's your job to tell her parents. I won't tolerate that type of behavior. She has to go."

Bargaining for time to think, I said, "Let me think about how I can do that. Her parents are just like you. They're just a hard-working couple. Perhaps I can speak with her directly."

This approach didn't sit well with him. He became more belligerent as he stood there.

Finally, I said, "This is your personal problem. I'm not a referee. If you can't handle this yourself, you should move out. I'll gladly refund your deposit. I can't afford to have this kind of behavior here. This is a very respectable place."

This infuriated him. I thought for a moment he was going to slug me. By the time he left, I was trembling — in part from anger and partly due to my carnal thoughts about the precocious girl. In time, I forced the accuser and his family to leave, which created a lot of pain for me. The bastard called the owners and told them his story. They called me. "Why are you siding with the girl? Her family is just here for the summer. This man signed a contract for one year with options to renew."

"Well, this couple had lived here when the previous manager was here, so I called the ex-manager and asked him what he could tell me about the family filing the complaint"

"What did he tell you?"

"He said he had the same issues with the father and finally just evicted them."

"Go ahead and evict them. Just make sure you document the incident in case we get sued over it."

I evicted the family and the son-of-a-bitch called the owners and told them I called their mother a "tight ass Jew." I loved the woman he was talking about. She was the classiest woman in Austin and without a pretentious bone in her frail body. It made me sick to my stomach.

One of my more memorable moments at the complex was when a tenant called and said, "The people downstairs are making so much noise we can't even watch TV."

I knew the couple who lived in the apartment. Howell and I had worked together at Senator Ralph Yarborough's campaign headquarters. I thought to myself, "He'll understand."

I noticed a black Lincoln Continental illegally parked in front of the walkway leading to their apartment. I thought it was someone who had just stopped in to say hello. I knocked and Howell came to the door.

"Hey Ray, come on in. We got one hell of a poker game going here. Let me introduce you. This is John Connelly and his girlfriend. John is a law student at UT."

I recognized the name immediately. It was Governor Connelly's son. John the Third looked like a soap opera star. Tall, well groomed, black hair, and probably 6' 3". Seemed like a hell of a nice guy.

"Howell, I would love to play poker. Unfortunately, I'm here to relay a message from your upstairs neighbors. They called about the ruckus you guys were creating. Can you keep it down?"

So much for my 15 minutes of fame. I never saw John again. I always suspected he deserted the Democratic Party as his father had done.

Social Work, Politics, and Strange Bedfellows

I graduated in December. From June '66 to Dec. '69, I had earned a degree. Not counting the year I spent at the feed yard and in recovery, it had taken just over two and a half years. I was crazy as a loon by now. My brain was sizzled from speed, morphine, and sleep deprivation. I was still wearing my leg brace but the radial nerve in my arm healed completely and I could use my left arm again.

The tough schedule took its toll on my mental state. Driven by the conflagration in my head ignited by excessive doses of speed, I was led to believe I was indefatigable. So I added to the insanity by becoming very active in social causes. Dr. Witherspoon, dean of the UT Law School, invited me to teach at the Citywide Committee for Human Rights. Major corporations from our local conglomerate giants such as Tracor and IBM volunteered their under-utilized executives as administrators and teachers. I had pretty much made up my mind by this time to study law at UT. I thought my association with Dr. Witherspoon would serve me well.

Working with the poorest minorities from east Austin was as gut-wrenching as working with the mentally handicapped children at the Texas State School. One student told Dr. Witherspoon, the school director, that getting to class was a major obstacle. A female student was raped while waiting for the bus. Another student was robbed. Others were harassed for attending a "honkie" establishment. Excuses for absences were not the usual "I wasn't feeling well," but something much worse.

Both Kari and I taught at the center. It was a great experience, but exasperating. I met the movers and shakers in the business and academic community. Equally important, I met and befriended some of the most deprived people in Austin. My students adopted Kari and me into their community. Some Saturdays I would visit east Austin in the hope of running into a student. Most whites avoided east Austin like the plague. It was not a safe place, even by daylight. Men walked the streets, purveying skinned raccoons. Some of the barkers offered me choice cut steaks stolen from the county hospital's loading dock just hours before. In spite of their unorthodox ways, I loved these people. Their lifestyles and moral values were certainly different from my own, but that didn't keep me from connecting with them.

In addition to soliciting my wife as a voluntary teacher, I enlisted a very well built girl from St. Edward's. Martha was a voluptuous vixen from Chicago. We fell in heat. One weekend we fled to Mexico for a two-night stand.

Martha argued with me most of the way to Del Rio, probably out of anxiety. We both had a full understanding of what we were about to do. We wasted no time in getting in bed when we arrived at the motel. I mounted her like a stud horse, but I couldn't get inside her. "Shit," I thought, "she's a virgin." I gave her a chance to back out.

"This is going to hurt. Are you sure you want to?"

"Yes. I have an inverted womb." she said. "Just shove it in. I'll hold my breath. I'll be okay."

It wasn't as difficult as I'd thought it would be, but it was pure hell for her. Made me wonder why a woman would ever have sex.

I don't know why, probably the speed in my body, but we had sex for three hours, dismounting only for piss calls. She fell in love. She must have had a dozen orgasms that night. The next day she wouldn't even eat. Love can kill one's appetite.

She loved me and held my hand tightly as we strolled through the streets of Del Rio, as if to say, "You are mine now." The trip back to Austin was quiet. She wanted to go back to the motel and do it all over again. I did too, even though I was exhausted. I don't think I could have lasted for ten minutes, let alone three hours. But I sure wanted to try.

Kari stood staring out the bedroom window awaiting my return. Filled with remorse, I parked and went upstairs, only to meet my very depressed wife. My heart ached from shame. It surged through my soul. She was pregnant with our second child. There she stood, wearing the navy blue maternity dress her mother had sewn for her. We couldn't afford a store-bought outfit — yet I could afford a 400-mile excursion to Del Rio. She was so precious in that dress. She only wore it on special occasions. I had told Kari I was going to Del Rio to write a story about the emerging Latino political party. My returning home must have been her reason for dressing up.

Nevertheless, Martha and I continued to spend at least one day a week together. She liked making love, and so did I.

Martha had a turquoise ring which she'd left at the motel in Del Rio. The motel sent it to my home address. Kari opened the box and found the ring.

"Whose ring is this?" she asked.

"Oh, I think its Brother David's. He rode down with me. I'll give it to him tomorrow."

I returned the ring to Martha the next day. Little did I know, she would show up at my house wearing the damn thing.

One night she and her roommate came to our apartment to play cards. She was wearing her turquoise ring.

"I have seen that ring before," Kari told Martha. "Is it yours?"

Martha replied, "Yes."

"That is strange. It sure looks like the one the motel sent to Ray."

So went the evening — a barb sent, a barb returned. By the end of the night, I was sick to my stomach. Somehow, I had to rectify my sins against my God and Kari.

A fundamental change was taking place, both in my belief system and my personality. Not only could I feel it — I could sense it. Prior to my NDE, I would never have thought that I would be unfaithful to my sweet wife. If someone had told me I would ever cheat on Kari, I would have knocked his lights out. Yet, here I was in the middle of an extramarital relationship.

Martha told her roommate about our night of perpetual sex. Shortly thereafter, her roommate came to our apartment just as Kari was heading out to teach. Mary said, "I just want to die. I tried slitting my wrist. It didn't work. See my wrist? If only I could escape for a few hours, I would be okay."

I knew exactly what she wanted. I took her to the bedroom, where we engaged in foreplay for thirty minutes. Finally, I lifted her dress and was about to remove her panties, when my conscience kicked in. I couldn't go through with it. Also, I knew if I did, there would be other girls showing up the next night.

Martha obviously found out that Mary came to my apartment. I always suspected Martha and Mary had preplanned the meeting — just to test me. All hell broke loose. Our relationship really got nasty. I went to her dorm one afternoon to talk with her. When she saw me standing at the door, she flipped me off, turned around and casually walked towards her room. She had borrowed some books from me and never returned them. So I asked her roommate, Mary, to bring the books to me at school. I got the books back all right, but not at school and not by Mary; they came to my home by way of the USPS, COD. The books were in the box, all right, along with four red bricks. Kari received the package and opened it to see what was inside. I don't recall how or even if, I explained my way out of that one.

Mary and I continued to be friends long after my tryst with Martha. Martha, of course, played the "woman scorned" role and I never saw her again. I assume she dropped out of college and returned to her home in Chicago. I have no idea how our relationship would have played out if she had not opted to leave, but I can honestly say I am happy it ended. "How in hell did I get in that mess," I mused.

As awful as I felt about my extramarital affair with Martha, I fell into another fling — and then another, and another. I always felt that I was a homely person — big nose, big ears, gap-toothed. Yet, women seemed attracted to me — as I was to them. Most near-death experience people report that they became more sensitive to the needs of others. Not so for me — unless they were females and their needs were for sex.

Highs and Lows

Still reeling from my illicit relationships, the devastating impact both on my body and in my brain from years of crank, I reached a euphoric high about graduating. I had made it through college - but what a price I paid. The net effect was insanity. Speed is known for producing extreme highs and subsequent lows — the definition of bipolar disorder?

Kari and I received money from the insurance company that covered the manufacturer of a faulty metal piece the hospital installed on my femur. Part of the insurance money went towards clothing for the both of us, the rest we used to buy more houses. The bulk we invested in stocks. Brilliant investors that we were, it must have taken three whole months to lose it all.

Two of my former professors encouraged me to attend graduate school instead of law school. One wanted me to pursue history. The other thought I should get my MBA. Prior to deciding, I sat for the LSAT exam. With a law degree, I'd be able to break into politics.

During the six-hour exam, the UT band began blasting the air with "noise" — bugles, percussions, tubas, trombones, clarinets, tambourines, saxophones — everything they could carry. Damnedest cacophony of shit one could imagine. No one was playing from a book. Each was doing their own thing. There was no reason for the band to practice on Saturday, nor was there a reason to be practicing near the classrooms. They had the entire football field available to them.

The band assembled directly behind the building where we were taking the exam. Scores on the exam were horrible and erratic. Princeton offered to allow any student who had taken the exam to take it again, free. The test was such a challenge I swore I would never take it again. My grade was half of what it took for acceptance in the prestigious UT School of Law.

I'd banked some political capital over the past two years, it was now time to call in the favors. A friend of mine, with whom I had studied business law said, "I'll call Dr. Witherspoon and see if he can waive the requirements."

I reminded him I also knew Witherspoon well and had worked under him at the Citywide Committee for Human Rights. But the Dean was uncompromising. He refused to waive the test score requirements for entrance.

As a consolation prize for past service at the Community Center, Dr. Witherspoon arranged for me to serve as Democratic Chairman for Precinct One. I jumped at the chance. It met my primary objective for wanting a law degree to begin with — it gave me an opportunity to get into politics. During the next six months, I worked my ass off to gain their respect. I quickly assembled a team of volunteers and began canvassing everyone in my precinct.

The presidential candidate was George McGovern. Additionally, the party supported a plethora of county, city and state candidates. I distinguished myself as an organizer and a person with a flair for politics.

Kari and I began receiving invitations to every political rally, fundraiser, and private gathering at the top-seeded democrats' homes. Amphetamines were no longer required to maintain a high. Being in the midst of the most widely-known politicians was all the stimulant I needed. Again, I felt it was divine intervention. How else could one explain my success?

With a little help and encouragement from my political friends, and several thousand dollars I received from the insurance company as a result of the accident at the feed yard, I purchased three more houses, all with no down payment. This was a far cry from my undergraduate days when I couldn't afford an $87 mortgage payment. There was no shortage of prospects to rent the homes. Place an ad one day, and collect the money the next.

A Run for Mayor

In the heat of the contest to persuade me to enter history or business, Dr. Osterhaus, Dean of the business department at St. Edwards, offered me a teaching assistant position that included; free tuition and a little money. In essence, I served as his secretary. He was an ex-military officer, with a PhD from UT in Hospital Administration. He had a fantastic brain — he wrote many articles for trade magazines and scholastic journals. I was lucky to work for him.

My euphoria ran rampant. I had met all the politicians. Some provided a little assistance with my real estate loans, but not one of them helped me find a job. Oh sure, they each wanted me on their team — but only as a volunteer.

So I ran for Mayor of Austin. The recognition would surely catch some employer's attention. My metabolism surged, I had energy to spare, and this time it didn't come in the form of a pill. This was my chance to shine. I ran on an environmental platform — Green Peace was popular with the intellectuals and young people — but it was acid for the establishment. I counted on winning the students' votes. Wrong! Students were non-residents.

The press backed me. They treated me like a seasoned office holder. Rick Fish, a City Desk reporter for the Austin Statesman, covered my campaign, taking pictures along the way and writing articles in support of my campaign. Rick was murdered in Dallas some years later. What a friend he was.

It should be no surprise that I was a miserable failure as a candidate — great as an organizer, but lousy as a candidate. On April 3, 1971 I received 750 votes out of a voting population of 75,000. That was the most degrading experience I had ever suffered — and still is, fifty years later. Humiliating, to say the least.

There I was in graduate school, up to my ass in shit I had never heard of before. I had just lost my election bid. I was completely disgraced and lost. Yet, due to my status as the Dean's TA, the professors gave me passing grades. Most of our graduate professors also taught at UT. UT's policy was to give no grade lower than a "B" for graduate students. I made a lot of "B"s.

I met a fellow student who told me of an open position as an auditor for the state Education Department — the same division Kari had worked for since arriving in Austin. I still had two semesters of graduate school remaining. I thought "What the hell? I can quit my night job now." I applied and got the job. Now I was making the best money in my life — $900 per month — but it was quite a step down from working on major political campaigns and running for a public office.

Extensive travel was required. As a rule, Monday was a travel day, as was Friday; we would return to Austin for weekends. However, if it was less expensive to house us in motels near our client's location than to pay mileage for our round-trip return to Austin, we spent the weekend away from home.

Road trips, especially those requiring weekend stay-overs, fit me to a "T." I drank every night, and pursued every female I could find — both at our clients' establishments and at local dance halls and pubs. Discretion was simply not a part of my thinking. I never used a condom — thankfully I never contracted an STD. My co-workers were, for the most part, just like me — drinkers and skirt chasers. Prior to my NDE accident, I was nothing like this. I went from loyal and trustworthy to a liar, drunk and womanizer. The change in my behavior baffled me — but didn't stop me.

It took a year, but they finally promoted me to field auditor for an entitlement program. Field auditors traveled to a client's office and reviewed their expenditures to ensure the organization was in compliance with state and federal requirements. I was their first auditor. That became a real cluster-fuck. I knew shit about "fund accounting". I searched for other people's mistakes. I crunched hundreds of numbers, hoping to find an irregularity I could nail them with. It didn't take long to get bored with that job. It was too detailed and structured for me. A year after beginning, I wanted out.

My father called and asked if I was interested in a job as manager for a custom butcher shop in Aspen, CO. At that time, Aspen might as well have been Timbuktu, but I wanted out of the auditing business, so without consulting Kari, I accepted the job. She agreed to stay behind while I went on to Aspen to build the store. She was to join me after the first of the year.

Off to Aspen

September 1972, five weeks after giving notice to my Manager at the State Auditor's office, I found myself driving over Independence Pass — sweating like a prizefighter battling Mohammed Ali. State Hwy 82 is a horrifying drive, nothing but switchbacks and steep drop-offs, a convoluted, treacherous road over the top of one of the steepest peaks in Colorado. I panicked all the way to the summit. At times, I pulled over to regain my composure. I thought I must have misunderstood my father about directions. Surely, no one in his right mind would use this road. At places, the bottom of the canyon must have been 2,500 feet below the paved road. No guard rails anywhere. I couldn't help but wonder what kept people from driving over the side? Later, I found out — nothing! One of Aspen's locals told me people go over the cliff several times a year.

Scared to death and drenched in sweat, I arrived in Aspen Village. It was nothing special, just some old stone buildings and a sprinkling of Victorian homes. "Why in the world would my father pick this place to build a retail meat market?" I asked myself.

The only common element was the people. Based on what I'd seen driving in, I was expecting to see these "gray" beings with little antenna.

There are simply too many differences between Austin and Aspen to describe them all. Austin had scrub oak and mountain cedar. Aspen was filled with fir, pine and Aspen trees. Austin was bumper to bumper driving – Aspen I don't recall ever having seen a traffic light. The kids from both towns dressed in blue jeans and bib coveralls. Aspen had 95 restaurants and 1,700 Aspenites. Austin had 250 restaurants for 250,000 residents. Austin's night life was mostly confined to a few blocks of Sixth Street; the entire village of Aspen was a party place.

University of Texas Campus Parking
http://www.utexas.edu/maps/

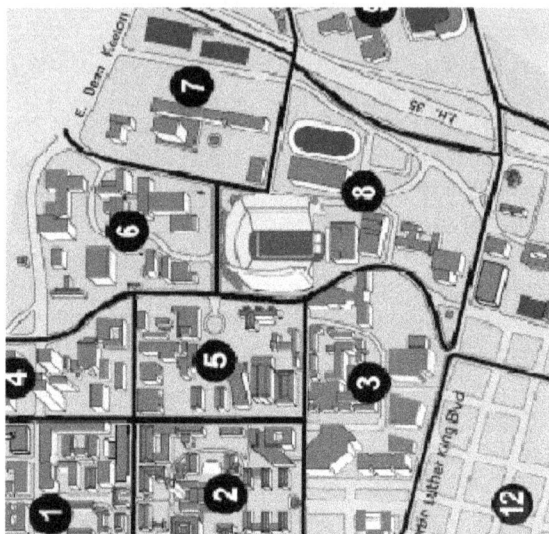

ASPEN COLORADO STREET MAP
http://www.ask.com/maps?sa=+++As pen%252C+CO&qsrc=

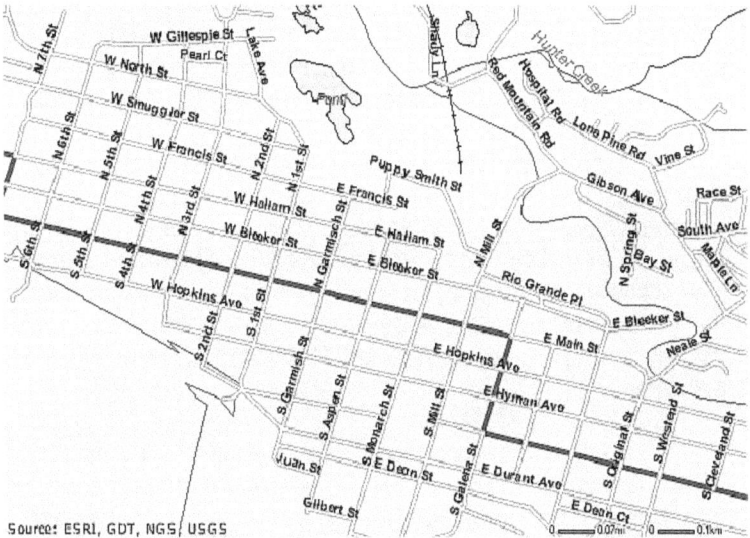

Source: ESRI, GDT, NGS, USGS

I searched the small community for my apartment — which didn't take long. I found the Aspen Square Building. Scherer, the building manager, welcomed me to Aspen. He handed me the keys to my condominium on the second floor and to my vacant shop in the lower level. The previous tenant had been the United States Post Office. I unloaded my car and took a tour of my new home. Great view — small quarters.

By the time I was through lugging my belongings up two flights of stairs, I was lightheaded. "I must have caught the flu," I thought to myself. A beer and some chicken soup should cure that. I meandered across the street to the local grocery. Again, I felt like I was going to pass out. I picked up a case of Heineken, some breakfast items and, of course, my chicken soup.

A six-pack later, I mustered the energy to tour my new shop. The space was fairly large by Aspen standards, but totally devoid of any appeal. My heart sank. Entering the shop from the street required walking down five steps. The walls were dingy from years of use — not to mention the yellow hue from decades of tobacco smoke. It seemed that everyone in Aspen smoked Marlboros. I never figured out why.

I retired to my condo where I sketched an outline of what I envisioned for the shop. The next morning I found a hardware store and purchased some basic tools and supplies. "How in the hell am I going to have this place ready for the ski season in November?" I pondered.

Remodeling began immediately. First, I sanded the handrails on the entry platform, working in spurts. I was still lightheaded. I could only work for three hours at a stretch, with fifteen minute breaks every hour. By the end of the first day, I could see some progress — kind of like digging a trench. I took refuge at the condominium after laboring for a few hours. I was sure I had some horrible dread disease. No one had warned me about altitude sickness before I arrived. A few red beers later and I just wanted to sleep — which I did.

From alligator shoes and three-piece suits, to mudder boots, red Bandanas, Pendleton wool shirts, blue jeans and a down jacket — all within a month. What a transition in life style. The small-town atmosphere reminded me of my own home town, where everyone knew and trusted each other.

I noticed when I moved in to my condominium that each patio, even those three stories up, had an ample supply of wood for the fireplace. It puzzled me. How did they get it up three stories? I knew they didn't climb the stairs with it under their arms. I caught them in action one afternoon. They parked their truck beside the building and tossed the wood, one log at a time, to the lowest patio. The man on that patio then tossed it up to the next and so on until all patios had a supply of wood.

I had a little more energy the following day. I attacked the stair rails with renewed vigor. For the first time in six years, I had abandoned speed as a crutch. I had quit too soon. I could have used a hit. I accomplished a great deal that day, but still felt dizzy. A few of the locals would drop by daily to find out what I was building. Dede Brinkman was one of the first. Her name meant nothing to me at that time, but she had a hot body. I made a mental note of her. Later someone told me she was a long-time local. Locals were a rare commodity. There were only 1,700 locals to serve the 100,000 tourists who came to Aspen each week.

One evening weeks later, after a night of heavy drinking, I lit my fireplace. There is nothing as enchanting as the smell of aspen wood burning in the fireplace. Sometime during the night, the wind began blowing. Next morning, I had a coating of ash about an eighth of an inch thick all over the condominium. What a mess. Another lesson learned.**New Friends with Benefits**

I called Kari nearly every day to bring her up to date on my progress. Damn, I missed my family. She had to care for two small children and still work for the Texas Education Department by day. Kari never complained. It wasn't her style. I didn't have much social life at that period in my life — and I believe she actually felt a sense of relief. Since my accident and the subsequent death of our first child, my personality had morphed into somewhat of a monster — full-time drinker and part-time womanizer. Deep down, I knew Kari could sense the dramatic change in my behavior.

After a week or two in Aspen, I was up to eight hours a day. I was a regular at the local pubs. My drinking put me in contact with all the local workers, and not a few pretty women. One such contact owned a carpet shop. Another was a carpenter, quite skilled in laying ceramic tiles. My favorite was a general contractor, Steve Wendell. Steve had a very dynamic personality. His father had amassed a fortune wildcatting in Oklahoma oil and gas ventures. Like so many young people in Aspen, Steve received a sizable check each month from a trust fund.

Soon the store's equipment arrived from Kansas. One piece was so damn large we couldn't get it through the doors. I asked Steve for help.

"Not a problem! I have a carpentry crew working on a condominium complex. They can come help you move that meat display. Just buy them a case of beer." The next day, a pickup arrived with a load of carpenters in the back. One of the crew, Bear, as he was known, told his crew, "Remove the front window. We'll move it in through there."

This scared the shit out of me. That is the last thing I would have recommended. But far be it from me to tell this motley crew how to do their job. Within ten minutes, the display was in the shop. Fifteen minutes after that it was in place. The two cases of Olympia beer didn't last long. Needless to say, Steve became a life-long friend.

Another drinking buddy, P.J., offered to lay the ceramic tiles. "P.J, I want tiles on the walls as well — about six feet high. I want to be able to steam clean the entire place, walls included, at the end of each day. Cleanliness is essential for a retail shop purveying food."

Within two days, P.J. gathered a crew and began work. He even selected the color of tiles. By Friday, he was through.

"I can't believe my luck," I mused. "Rather be lucky than talented."

Lastly, I bumped into another artisan and shop owner, Stephan. He owned an upscale rug company at the airport complex.

Stephan told me, "I can install the carpeting. Something rustic would go well. Maybe a brown, with burnt-orange, indoor-outdoor, shallow-nap?"

He was spot on. His selection nailed the décor I wanted to present. By the time he completed the installation, the place looked like a million dollars. Together, my friends had captured the true feeling of Aspen — we had one of the nicest shops in town, no matter what was sold there. I glowed with pride. From then on, people would come by just to see the remarkable transformation — from an old post office to a truly remarkable restoration.

Later that summer, I met Steve's girlfriend's father. Steve and Joy lived in a teepee beside a mountain lake. They had two children. Joy's father came by my shop, to shoot the shit one afternoon. He was wearing a plaid jacket that stuck out like a neon light in a thunderstorm. He had to tell me about his stay in the teepee — perhaps just to see my reaction. I could tell he was shocked about their bizarre living quarters.

"I spent the night with Steve and Joy up on the lake. Did you know they lived in a genuine teepee? I would never have believed it, but we all were able to bed down inside. Hell, the outdoors was their restroom. They bathed in the lake. That is where I drew the line. It was below freezing this morning. Here they were running around naked, bathing in the frigid water. They at least warmed the bath water for the babies."

Much later, I discovered his identity. He owned one of the largest ranches in Texas. Joy, his daughter, was a "trust-fund child," as was Steve. My father, a cattleman all his life, knew of Joy's family but had never met them. He was envious as hell.

"I need to meet him. Can you arrange it?" But it was not to be. I never saw Mr. McLaughlin again.

Steve and Joy were two of the wealthiest people I had met — and both were friends. They didn't have a pretentious bone in their bodies. "It doesn't get any better than this," I thought. "Aspen is turning out to be a dreamland." It was like a mirage, a beautiful oasis nested among majestic mountains.

Over time, I became acquainted with almost all of the permanent residents, or locals as they were known. The static population was about 1,700 — most of them day laborers and wait-staff in the ninety-five local restaurants; the rest were trust fund kids.

Mutual Support

My first season had come and gone. Aspen had two seasons: "off season" and "in season." During the off season, one could go to lunch and leave his shop door open. People looked after one another. They might "borrow" from you but they weren't going to steal. I'd go to the shop early in the morning and prepare sandwiches for the day workers and then I'd go fly fishing near Ashcroft, leaving prepared sandwiches on top the meat display cooler. Soft drinks and chips were in another cooler. I used a cigar box as my "cash box." Customers left their money in the box, or their IOU. Andre, owner of the legendary Andre's Club, told me "Take good care of the locals. When the tourists leave town, the locals will be your only source of income." I followed his advice. The shop was now well-founded and prosperous.

Steve Wendell came by to tell me that he and Joy were going to Australia for a week or so. A month later and the two of them were still gone. I began to think something had happened to them. His carpentry crew (some of my best sandwich customers) came by my shop.

"Ray, we haven't heard from Steve in over a month. He didn't leave any money for our salaries. Shit, we don't have the money he does. We have to feed our families and pay our rent. Have you heard anything from him?"

"No. I haven't. I've been sort of worried about him myself. Can I help you guys in any way? I can't pay your salaries, but might be able to open an account for you. Would that help?"

"Ray, you are a life saver. You are the newest member in Aspen and the most generous. What do we need to do to open an account?"

I handed them a book of sales receipts and told them to sign a receipt for whatever they took and stick the receipt in the cigar box I kept near the register.

It worked out great. They came by the shop each morning to pick up their sandwiches while I was out on the river trout fishing. I'd check my cigar box upon return just to see if they had made it in. I could count on their crew to buy a dozen sandwiches each morning and about the same at noon.

These guys were the same ones who had moved my equipment in through the window when I first opened. I was forever indebted to them. I began stashing cases of beer inside my walk-in meat cooler for them as well. To this day, any one of them would give me the shirt off his back.

Steve and Joy arrived home early June. I assumed Steve caught a lot of flak from his crew. He came by my shop and said, "Ray, I hear my crew ran up some debt with you in my absence. How much do I owe you?" He wrote me a check on the spot for the full amount and thanked me repeatedly.

All I can say is that it must be damn nice to have as much discretionary money as he and Joy had.

Steve, an avid skier, came by my shop nearly every day on his way to Ajax Mountain. He would do this little dance, emulating a skier plowing through a mogul field, and wave me to follow. He was a hoot. I never saw Steve out on the town in the evening. Come to think about it, I never saw him smoke a joint.

Steve included me in some of his most lucrative real estate deals. One such deal was a 640-acre ranch owned by a pharmacist in California. The owner wanted $640/acre — a steal even in those days. The place came with a house, smoke house and several sheds. The Roaring Fork River, popular with local trout fishermen, ran through the entire length of the property. Steve laid out a plan to break up the ranch into individual tracts. Each tract had access to the river. He was a genius. I called my father and a few political contacts back in Austin to borrow the money. But before I could find my share of the deal, the land sold to another buyer.

On another occasion, Steve offered me a new condominium at the base of Little Nell. He had built a beautiful condominium complex, the outside made of basalt, mined from the mountain near Old Snowmass. He said, "Ray, I have one unit left. I need to sell it. Give me $82,000 and it's yours." I couldn't raise the cash. Today that same condominium is worth in excess of $2M. I don't think Steve knew I lived from paycheck to paycheck. It was the thought that counted. I shall never forget Steve.

Awesome Aspen Night Life

Night after night, I would go to one establishment or another, until I became close friends with the majority of the restaurant and shop owners, as well as their employees. Word of my generosity with Steve's crew had spread throughout town. I was justifiably elated. It was indeed a dreamland. I couldn't go anywhere in town without someone inviting me to join in whatever festivities were at hand. Such recognition only fired my ego. After awhile, I was right back in my old manic way of life.

Aspen in the '70s was a bit like Woodstock. Everyone carried a stash of weed and most had some blow, or at least knew someone who would share. I never much cared for weed; it made me feel nauseated, particularly if my system was loaded with alcohol. Now cocaine was a different story. Cocaine had a sobering effect. A couple of beads in the morning after a hard night of boozing, and I was good for the day. Locals bartered in cocaine. Rich folks served it in candy bowls. It was everywhere. Some used it because it was sociable, others because it was allegedly an aphrodisiac.

Bill Cosby is quoted as having quipped, "I said to a guy, 'Tell me, what is it about cocaine that makes it so wonderful?' And the guy said, 'Well, it intensifies your personality.' And I said, 'Yes, but what if you're an asshole?'" That was me.

Cocaine, booze, and power bred a perfect "asshole" in my own case. I transformed into a full-blown megalomaniac. "Welcome home, asshole. What took you so long?" I heard a voice from within say.

The new ski season was just beginning, but the Arabs cut off fuel supplies to the United States and vacationers were having trouble finding gasoline. The season got off to a horrible start. We were struggling to make enough money at the shop to pay the employees. I was losing cash every day.

My father sent four women from Wichita, Kansas to stay at my apartment during their ski vacation. All were married to doctors. Their husbands were friends of his. When you live in Aspen, every person you ever met over the years calls as a "friend" hoping to get free lodging for a week. Maybe that's what these upper-middle-class women wanted, or maybe not. They might have just wanted to be on the "in" for a week. It was a high-status thing to be introduced around town by a local.

I picked them up at the airport. They were dressed in their Russian fur hats, mink Eisenhower jackets, and calf-high furry boots. The locals wore blue jeans and wool shirts and après ski wear. I thought, "Oh well. I've seen worse."

We went to the nearest bar to unwind (and so I could size them up). One of them, Gloria, was a hot mama. Unlike the others, she was not a grandmother. She had two pre-adolescent girls. The other three were my mother's age. Two drinks at 8,600 feet up are sufficient to get a real buzz for most "flat-landers." My ladies were no different. All four were drunk and rowdy within an hour of stepping off the plane.

We drove the three miles back to my abode, where I had a roast simmering. The smell of the cooking food was enough to send anyone's taste buds into convulsions. They ate the entire pot of roast and vegetables at one setting. They raved about it. "This is the best roast I ever tasted."

A couple more rounds of drinks, and we retired for the night. Around midnight I woke up with a hard on. My philosophy is that an erection is a terrible thing to waste. Still a bit tipsy, I began rationalizing. "Should I or not? What if one of them screams when I approach her? Which one shall I hit on? Will word get back to my father? Will the one I proposition go tell the other three?"

It didn't take long to make my decision. Not once did I think that the best choice was to do nothing. Not once. The difference between a sick mind and a sane one is not the desires and fantasies; it's that the sick ones act on those desires.

"I'll try the blonde one with the two girls. She is the hottest."

I crept to Gloria's bed and placed my hand on her breast. Just as I thought, she sat straight up to a sitting position and stared at me as if to say, "What in the hell are you doing?" Before she could ask, I whispered, "Let's go to my bedroom."

A broad toothy smile nervously crossed her confused face. We tip-toed across the hall to my bedroom with pajamas and negligees flying in all directions. We hopped into bed — it took about thirty seconds. No foreplay required. We went straight to sex, and she wore my ass out. I was nodding off. She whispered in a muted tone, "I'd better return to my bed before one of them notices I'm missing."

Just as I had thought, the next evening, two of the older women began groping me in front of the others. For a while I thought they were going to rip my clothes off and rape me — it wouldn't have taken much effort. I managed to divert their unsolicited attention long enough to fix drinks and something to eat. I was anxious for everyone to get to sleep so I could get Gloria back in bed.

She was a good lay and a horny one at that. Just my type of girl. I guess I performed too well — Gloria fell in love with me. She became very protective, even when we were out on the town. Gloria was scaring all my local girlfriends away. I didn't mind her showering affection on me around her friends (that might keep them off my ass) but around my steady lays, now that was a bit over the top. The four were returning home at the end of the week and I had to live there day-in and day-out.

My friend Steve Naumberg volunteered to help me entertain them. Steve was a member of the ski patrol, and his lot never lacked for women. But these women were too old for Steve — he liked the tight teenagers. Nevertheless, he didn't let on if he was bored with them.

We drank until we couldn't walk, then Steve broke out the dope. Weed on top of whiskey generally made me sick as hell. However, I jumped right into the fray. We had a good ole time, until one of the gals got the dry heaves. She started slipping in and out of consciousness. Steve took her outside. I assumed they were out for a fuck. It was ten degrees below zero and there was at least three feet of snow in the yard.

Half an hour later, one of the others wanted to go check on her. I tagged along just to see what the hell was taking them so long. Much to our surprise, Steve had dug a snow bed and covered her in a blanket of snow to help sober her up. They both had their clothes on.

For the first time, I saw another side of Steve. Beneath his cavalier persona, he was a loving and caring gentleman. This was a noble deed, in my eyes. That solidified our friendship. We remained close friends for the rest of my days in Aspen, and years thereafter. But me? Sit outside in the freezing snow for thirty minutes just to comfort a drunk? No way!

Hot Load

So much for my horny house guests. They had come for a good time, and a good time they had. It was a once-in-a-lifetime event for most of them. They returned to Wichita that weekend. I can't say I missed their company. However, they had entertained me as much as I had them. Now it was time to gather my harem back together, the ones I had to live with every day. I couldn't afford to alienate any one of them — nights were too cold to sleep alone.

Spring skiing was just beginning and I needed to replenish my inventory, so I took off for Kansas, where the IBP warehouse was located. I called Gloria and told her I was coming through Wichita that evening. I drove straight through from Aspen. I was so tired when I got in that I was like a punch drunk. I went to the bar for a nightcap before retiring. The bar at the hotel was loaded with doctors from all over the country. They were in town for a convention. I struck up a conversation with a couple of pediatricians from Mexico. It was if we had known one another for years. We were having a great time. I soon forgot how tired I was. One drink turned into a half dozen. About the time I was ready to turn in I felt a tap on my shoulder.

"Hey, sailor. Want to have some fun?" I knew that voice. I whirled around on my barstool. There stood Gloria. She only had one thing on her mind — sex. I had no idea how I was going to make love when I was so dog tired and about three sheets to the wind. Off to the room we ran. She fucked me like a hired hand for an hour, until I couldn't take any more. She said, "Mind if I take a sitz bath before I go home?"

"No. Please, feel free."

"We were entertaining earlier, or I would have come sooner. When the guests left, I jumped up and told my husband I was going out. I left the dirty dishes and silverware soaking in warm water."

"Where did her husband think she was going?" I thought. "Did he follow her? Did he know any of the doctors I met in the lounge? Probably so. Oh well. Let chance work it out."

I walked her down to the hotel entrance, hand in hand. She hugged me warmly and kissed me like there was no tomorrow. I had experienced that behavior before with Martha in Austin. It scared me. She was acting like a teenager in love.

"Can I see you tomorrow?" she asked.

"Sure. Why don't you join me for breakfast?"

"I have to take the girls to school at 8:00. It will be around 8:30 to 9:00 before I get here."

"That's alright. I'll be ready," I assured her.

She jumped into her black Mercedes convertible and sped off into the night. I couldn't stop thinking about what her husband was going to say or do when she got home. Would they argue? Would he beat her? Where was she going to tell him she'd been? Maybe he just didn't give a shit! Eventually I fell asleep.

Next morning I got up early enough to shower, shave, change clothes, and check out before Gloria arrived. I was waiting at the valet station when she arrived. "Get in" she said.

We held hands while she sped away, driving with one hand, and groping me with the other. She never took her eyes off me.

"Where are we going?" I asked. "I thought we were having breakfast."

"To my house."

"Oh shit. All her neighbors are going to see us?" I thought.

She didn't care. It was if she wanted to show me off to her friends. We arrived at a huge one story, sprawling ranch style home. She clicked the garage door opener and drove into the garage. She couldn't wait to show me her entire house. She apologized for all the dirty dishes still cluttering the dining room table.

"Doesn't her husband care?" I thought.

After some serious sex, I told her I had to get to the packing plant in Salina before they closed. She was very quiet on our drive back to the hotel. She looked like she had just lost her best friend. I suspect she sensed we wouldn't meet again.

After Gloria dropped me off, I traded my rental car for a Ryder truck. I dreaded this leg of the trip. The land was barren; just some sage brush bushes. I arrived at the warehouse about 6:00 p.m. and immediately ran into trouble. The dockhand refused to load my truck. It was not refrigerated.

"The meat will rot before you reach Aspen," he told me.

"Listen to me, prick. That's not your concern. When the meat is on my truck, it's mine. If it rots, it rots. It's not your decision. Load me up and throw dry ice on top of the load."

By the time we finished arguing I had lost an hour of valuable time. It was dark and I had one hell of a drive back through the mountains to Aspen. I realized I would have to drive straight through, with no time for sleep. My intentions were to travel at night to avoid the sun, but I was getting a late start. So much for my great planning. Off into the night I drove.

Something's Rotten

About sun-up, I arrived in Denver. The sun was blazing down on my load. "I may have five tons of cooked meat by the time I get to Aspen," I worried.

When I hit the mountains, a highway patrolman pulled me over. He scared the shit out of me. I was groggy from lack of sleep; I hadn't eaten in seventeen hours, and felt discombobulated. The officer ran me through the routine questions:

"What are you carrying?"

"Fresh red meat," I replied

Where are you coming from?"

"Wichita, Kansas."

"What is your destination?"

"Aspen."

"Well, you're still five hours away. It's not safe to drive so many hours."

"I didn't know there was a restriction on non-commercial trucks," I replied.

"There isn't. But you shouldn't tackle the mountains when you're tired."

"Officer, I don't want to sound disrespectful, but if I don't get this load of meat out of the sun and into my cooler soon, it's going to rot. Now may I get back on the road?"

"You're free to go. I'm calling ahead to alert the other officers. They'll pull you over during the remainder of your trip, as a courtesy. We just want to make sure you're capable of driving."

Sure as shit, about once an hour, a squad car would pull me over and chat with me. In retrospect, they did me a huge favor. There is no doubt in my mind that I was a time bomb. I could barely keep my eyes open and I was approaching some of steepest grades in the state. Some of the down slopes are so treacherous they build run-away ramps along the side for run-away trucks. It's not uncommon for a truck to burn out the brakes before getting to the bottom of the mountain. The only safe way is to gear down at the top of the mountain. I couldn't do that — not with an automatic transmission.

At that point, I really didn't care. "Just get my ass home," I kept thinking. With an abundance of grace from God, and a lot of courtesy stops by Colorado's finest, I pulled into Aspen around five in the afternoon. I gathered all my employees, except the cashier. We assembled a bucket brigade and off-loaded the warming meat into the walk-in cooler.

I informed Jan, my assistant manager, "I'm going to bed. Lock this freaking place up for me. I'll either see you at the apartment or tomorrow morning." Housing was expensive and in short supply in Aspen, so Jan stayed in one of my bedrooms. I picked up a case of beer at Adolph's liquor store and drove home. I could barely carry my own weight. No problem sleeping that night.

Next morning, I was healed and ready to resume my daily duties. I couldn't get my mind off the night spent with Gloria in Wichita. It bothered me then and it still bothers me forty years later. I guess the reason for my remorse had more to do with going inside her house the next day — a home is for family, not lovers.

It had been days since I had even thought about my family back in Austin. "What has become of my life?" I was living inside a whirlpool. "How do I pull myself out of this quagmire without hurting others in the process?" My head was reeling from all my affairs and the wheeling and dealing. Was there no end to all the insanity?

Family Ties

Steven, my oldest son, came to live with me the summer of '73. He was three at the time. Kari and our daughter were to come later. The trip to Aspen was his first trip on an airplane. Steven endured the trip like a seasoned traveler.

I moved from my condominium to a three-bedroom apartment in anticipation of my family's arrival. Steven and I had a blast. During the day he would come to the shop. The employees spoiled him to a fault. He rode with our delivery man when he had to make out-of-town deliveries to Glenwood Springs and Vail. He thought he was hot shit — and he was.

Soon thereafter, Kari and my daughter arrived. Kari began working for the shop. This worked fine for a while, but I felt uneasy.

"What if one of my girlfriends comes by? What excuse am I going to use?" I asked myself. My old personality broke through. I had to get her out of the shop before she screwed up my night life. Perhaps a marriage counselor could persuade her to keep away from my place of work. So we went to a marriage counselor. The counselor told us that a husband and wife couldn't work at the same place and remain married.

"You each need some time to yourself. Kari, keep out of the shop. Ray, if she comes into the shop for any reason other than to shop, throw her out."

That ended that conflict. The two of us got the message. By and by, Kari found us a house on Laurel Mountain, about two miles south of Aspen. It was a beautiful house with an awesome view — mountains on every side, a small pond across Highway 82, to the west, and aspen trees everywhere. Mostly upper-middle-class families lived on the mountain.

Steven began having some disturbing problems dealing with his friends and our employees. He was loud, rowdy and combative. We made an appointment to see a child psychologist, and she referred us to a government-funded school that had just opened. The school's specific goal was to deal with gifted and troubled children. The founder was one of our customers. Acceptance into the school was contingent on a referral by a medical professional. Of course, knowing the founder didn't hurt.

The school consisted of three geodesic domes. Entrance was through a rabbit hole at the top of one of the domes. One had to climb a set of stairs to get to the top. The administrative offices were accessible through a portal on the ground level. Inside the burrow were observation windows so the kids could look out to watch the wildlife. Sounds of the wilderness were piped in by way of dozens of microphones placed around the surrounding forest of aspen trees. I was envious of Steven's new dwellings. I grew up on a farm, working my ass off. When I was his age, I was rounding up, milking, and feeding cows. Here he was, going to a "by invitation only" school. It was a one-of-a-kind place.

The school took the children on outdoor excursions when weather permitted. They pitched camp along the way and ate wild game for lunch. They did a little cross country skiing, and discovered the wonderful countryside. The school was the perfect place for developing young minds.

We enrolled him in the fall of 1974, and all went well his first semester. Then the director of the school demanded the three of us come to the school for a candid discussion. We had no idea what it was supposed to be about. Perhaps they wanted to advance him. After all, he was very intelligent. Boy, were we surprised. Upon arrival, we found another child and mother there. "This can't be good," I thought.

No shit! It was not good news. It seems the other student, a little four-year-old girl, and Steven liked to play "doctor" in the presence of the staff and other children. He had never seen that behavior in his young life. "Where the hell did he pick up this conduct?" Kari blamed me. I blamed her. We jointly blamed the school. The director said, "That is not the end of the story. Yesterday, he called the bus driver a "farty-ass elephant."

"And where did he learn such language?" Kari asked.

We were in shock. Nevertheless, I secretly admired the little shit. After all, I was the ultimate skirt chaser. "A chip off the old block," I said to myself. I suspect Kari was thinking, "Like father, like son."

The school suspended Steven for two weeks. Both Kari and I worked full time during the day. "How are we to take care of Steven while we're at work? Who would have to make the sacrifice?" After much deliberation, I agreed to take him with me. He was one big distraction in the store. Our delivery man suggested a workable solution — Steven would accompany him on his deliveries. He drove to Vail every other day, delivering meat orders to restaurants. The drive from Aspen to Vail takes you through Glenwood Canyon, one of the most scenic roads in the area.

"Damn, what punishment for a disruptive pupil." I knew most kids would pay for "discipline" like that.

It was a struggle getting him to return to school when his probation ended. Kari and I relayed our thought to the school director, Bob. He was not amused at our observation. I didn't give a shit. It was true. The irony was undeniable. The very philosophy of the school was founded on working with gifted, talented and troubled children. And they couldn't handle Steven?

By the time we were in full season, I was a raving maniac. I reverted to my philandering ways. From November to April, 20,000 to 100,000 visitors swarmed into town each week for their annual ski vacation. Many were single women. But prior to taking on the new flock of gals, I just had to try a fling with one of my employees. She and her live-in boyfriend had been neighbors when we lived on Smuggler Mountain. Her boyfriend was my delivery person — yeah, the same one who volunteered to take Steven with him on delivery trips.

Kari had taken our Audi to Glenwood Springs to have a new windshield installed. She was late in returning. Jan volunteered to take care of the children until Kari returned. Our house had glass walls on two sides — one of which had a full view of our driveway. While I was engaged in foreplay with Jan, Kari rolled in. She saw everything and the shit hit the fan. We decided that it would be better for the children if she took them back to Austin. I watched them drive into the distance and wondered if I'd ever see them again.

Alone Again – Naturally

It was April of 1974 and my lack of willpower ran as rampant as the Rockies' spring flowers. My reputation as a womanizer spread far and wide. I formed a pact with Steve Naumberg to see just how many "scores" we could rack up... the loser buying a case of whiskey for the other. As a ski patrolman, Steve got to meet every female who hit the slopes. He was well known about town. He only used his first name, never his surname, even in the phone directory. When it came to pay up for the previous week, if I was running behind, I'd drive the streets in search of women, who were not difficult to find. Out-of-town women were seemingly attracted to Aspen's locals. I never understood why, but they certainly were eager to please. Perhaps they aspired to forge a permanent relationship. Little did they know, relationships didn't last long in Aspen.

One evening Steve had no women at his house. He asked, "Well? Where are they? Go round up a couple. I'll call some folks and we'll get a party going."

Away I went. I made one trip around the square and I spotted a duo outside of Andre's. "Hey! You guys want to party?"

"Sure. Where?"

"At my friend's house. Don't worry, there will be a houseful."

One was a student from Boulder and the other was her cousin from Belgium. Although they were not the usual knockouts, what they lacked in beauty they made up for in charisma.

They were awe-struck at Steve's Alpine-style home. Then they became quite animated. Their eyes darted from one person to another as if to size everyone up. It was Saturday night and the house was full. Steve introduced himself. He winked at me and said, "You bastard!"

I split the girl from Boulder away from the group and led her upstairs to Steve's loft. She was naked in a nanosecond. For a fairly common face, she sure had one hell of a body. She was yummy. I began at the top and worked my way down — way down. Almost immediately, she began moaning. The closer to orgasm, the louder the moaning. I put my hand over her mouth to muffle the groans and moans, which were echoing throughout the house. After thirty minutes or so, we settled down to some old fashioned sex. Then she began to moan again. I knew the moaning was a put-on — but those in attendance didn't. I'd slept with enough women to know when one is faking it. It was embarrassing to me, and I'm not easily embarrassed.

After an hour or so, we strolled downstairs. Everyone at the party had stopped dancing so they could listen. There they sat, with smirks on their faces, just waiting for us to come out of the room. Her cousin was shocked, or maybe just disgusted. She wanted to return to their cabin immediately. I assume she thought she was going to be raped, but rape wasn't part of the Aspen culture.

The next day, Steve asked one of my regular lays, who worked for Keith Hefner, (brother of Huge Hefner) just how long my dick was. Dawn told him, "Just long enough to get the job done. Why?" Steve relayed the story from the previous night. Dawn replied, "It's not about the size. It's the way he uses it." Steve never let me forget that night. If he told the story once, I bet he told it a dozen times around Aspen.

Adulterers Only

I lost track of the number of women we laid. It ran in the dozens. Not once did we get an STD. Now that is the luck of the Irish! At one time, Steve was sleeping with a sixteen-year-old while the girl's mother slept on a bed in the living room.

The mother asked me, "Are you sleeping with me tonight?" That was a bit too much, even for the likes of me. I bid her goodnight and left for home. On my way out, she hollered, "What's the matter? Am I so bad I make you sick?"

I don't think she actually wanted an answer. Next day, I was again in hot pursuit of the next fox.

I was known as a whoremonger — "the seducer." Bartenders fixed me up with single women sitting around the bar. I was good for business. So much so, the bartenders gave me free drinks just to draw women.

I was proud of my reputation. I was Aspen's poster child for deplorable behavior. Women came and went on a weekly basis — sometimes on a daily basis. My fame as an eligible bachelor and womanizing bastard spread outside the city limits of Aspen. By now, I had my "reputation" to uphold. There was no turning back. My philandering ways had become the talk of the town. I was a legend to some; to others a menace to society.

I got a call one day while working at my shop.

"Ray, I'm Vicki. I'm looking for my boyfriend. Have you seen him?"

"Listen, I don't even know you. How would I know your friend?"

"Do you ever come to Denver, Ray?"

"Not very often."

"Write down my telephone number. I'd like to meet you. Call me the next time you're in town."

What a strange call. It had "con job" written all over it. Be that as it may, she had tossed the gauntlet. I made it a point to go to Denver. After checking into a local Holiday Inn near the stadium, I called her. To my surprise, she sounded happy to hear from me. Perhaps this wasn't a con. We agreed to have dinner that evening. I drove to her house in one of the poorer sections of town and knocked on the door. A young hippy girl answered and invited me in.

"I'm here to see Vicki. Is she in?'

"You must be Ray. She's expecting you. Come on in."

A voice called out from upstairs, "Ray! I can't believe I am finally getting to meet you. Come on up."

I climbed the stairs to find Vicki changing the diaper on an infant. Vicki was a beautiful blonde-haired girl with light blue, piercing eyes. She was about my height, slim, with a sculptured body. I didn't say anything, but thought plenty. "Where's the father?" was the first thing that popped into my mind. I smiled and took a seat in a nearby rocker.

When she had finished, she kissed the baby and said, "See you tomorrow. Momma is going out tonight."

It was as I thought. She was married, with a child, just trying to get even with her husband.

Her marital status didn't matter to me. If she had a husband, he was not there at the time. Nonetheless, I got her out of the house as fast as I could, without sounding too anxious.

The evening was a whirlwind. Vicki had a vivacious personality and laughed a lot. Her smile looked as if it had been cast on her face. I couldn't wait to get her back to my room. She was every bit as good in bed as I had fantasized. I don't know why, but I never saw her again. Vicki was the one girl out of the many I had slept with that I might have taken home with me.

After Christmas, Gloria called from Wichita to inform me she was coming to see me. That was the last thing in the world I needed. Being the caring son-of-a bitch I was, I said, "Come on!"

She came to town dressed like a male peacock in heat. The only other woman in Aspen who dressed like her was Jill St. John. At this time, there were only three celebrities in town: Jill, Claudine Longet, and John Denver.

John and Claudine were fairly quiet, never creating a distraction — at least not in public. (In 1977, Claudine was charged with misdemeanor negligent homicide in the murder of my friend, Spider Sabich). Jill, on the other hand, had a reputation for being a bit belligerent and boisterous when inebriated. I am confident her behavior compared favorably to the rest of ours.

Gloria arrived to an Aspen she had never seen in the past — and probably wouldn't see in the future. The two of us became an item. After a week or so, she decided she had better get home and care for her children. By now she considered me her "toy boy." She had marriage on her mind. I quizzed her about her relationship with her husband to find out that he, like so many other doctors, was having an affair with his nurse.

Gloria liked running around the apartment nude. The first time I saw her naked, in the light, it freaked me out. She had three one-inch-high welts across her abdomen. I presumed they were stretch marks from her two previous pregnancies. They were so grotesque, it turned my stomach. If I ever had long-term romantic aspirations with Gloria, they were gone. It was all I could do to make love with her after that. However, other than those marks, she was a looker. Just having her on my arm was a good advertisement. She was a head-turner.

Towards the end of the season, Terry, her husband, showed up at my shop. He had his nurse with him. She was about as homely a woman as I had seen in quite some time.

"Ray, I left my parka with Jan. Do you know where she is?" Jan was the assistant manager at my store.

"No, doc, she no longer works for me. I haven't seen her in about a month. I heard she is living somewhere in Snowmass."

Without so much as a word, he turned and left the store with his nurse in tow. I think he only stopped in to intimidate me. It didn't work. I was poking his wife and there was not a thing he could do about it.

The last thing I needed was for my wife and parents to find out about my relationship with Gloria. My father attended high school with Dr. O'Connor, a close friend of Gloria's husband, Terry. Mother had gone to school with O'Connor's wife. And me, I was having an affair with one of the group of close-knit doctors.

Finally, it happened. Gloria's husband filed for a divorce. Dr. O'Connor's wife, who attended the divorce trial, informed my father about my fling. He told my mother.

My father had known about my countless affairs going all the way back to my high school years — some with married women, but mostly with fellow students. He was proud of me. When I used to chauffeur him around country, he'd send women to my room. I'm sure some were hookers. When I moved to Aspen, he came to see me regularly, primarily to get me to fix him up with some of my "girlfriends".

Mother thought I had lost my wits. After hearing about my affair with Gloria, she figured her fears were confirmed. Now, in her mind, I was certifiably insane. After all, I was married and had two children.

"I've got to change my ways," I said to myself — over and over again. But I couldn't stop womanizing any more than I could stop breathing. Sex was habit-forming. I just had to have another "fix." Eventually, sometime in my early sixties, I aged out of the sex thing — but by then, the damage was done. My wife had left me. My children forgot who their dad was, let alone where he was. All they knew was they no longer had a dad around the house.

End of an Era

The one-night stands went on over a regular basis. Shuttle buses unloaded in front of my store, bringing droves of women. From my shop, I leered through the front window as they stepped off. "This one is mine. This one Steve can have. Ah, I want that one too." And off I'd go again. Women in Aspen were like sand on the beach. They were everywhere.

By now I had befriended nearly everyone, including John Denver. When Jim Connor, a mutual friend of John's and mine, came to town to play at a local restaurant or club, he would stay at my house. JD would call me — early in the morning, just about daylight, looking for Jim. I guess John was an early riser. His wife, Annie, was just about the most genuine woman in Aspen. Cute, but not beautiful, and always very courteous. She didn't accompany John on his many trips to town. They lived in Starwood, high above the prying eyes of the curious public.

Bob Collins, a customer of mine, owned Don Giovanni's restaurant. He was the most widely known gay in town. His brother, Larry, was the bartender at the restaurant. He and his girlfriend lived with Bob at his home in Starwood. Bob asked me to rent a house from him. Being one of my best customers, I acquiesced. Now I had two homes to pay for.

Living close to JD had its advantages — the biggest one being a pick up line. When a woman asked, "Can I see your house?" I'd say, "Sure. Which one? The one at Starwood or the one on Laurel Mountain?"

"Starwood? Starwood! Can you see John's home from your place?"

"No. Too many trees. But he lives about half a mile down from us."

Now that was exhilarating! The drawback was the trip down the mountain back to town. Damn difficult when you are drunk — drive with one hand on the steering wheel and the other one over one eye to help focus.

My favorite home was the one on Laurel. Not only was it beautiful, it was warm, cozy and had a fantastic view of the skiers and the lake where the kayakers trained. It was a fantasy. I never tired of it. Even today, it brings back many fond memories.

Each passing day, I found myself deeper in debt. I missed my family so much, but I knew I could never return. The memories were still fresh in my wife's mind and they were not pleasant ones. My behavior was such that I knew it was best for the children to be apart from me. In retrospect, I realize the way I acted was a defense mechanism. One-night stands don't require commitment. Love them today, and never see them again. No one got a chance to see the "real" me.

Finally, Larry, Bob's brother, caught me one morning on my way to work. He said, "Ray. This town is not for the two of us. We're better than this. We should leave while we still have a soul and some self respect."

This was exactly one day after he introduced me to a woman at his bar. She was a disc jockey from Chicago — not much on looks, but then, what the hell, it was the evening. There's a country & western song that says women all get better looking at closing time. How true. Of course, she wanted to go to the Starwood house. We couldn't see the moon from my room, so we slept in a room on the west side of the house. She spotted on the sheets. I don't know if she was beginning her period, or if she was a virgin — I didn't ask. Larry and Ronda, his girlfriend, cleaned the room. He raised seven kinds of hell about the sheets. Maybe Larry just wanted me to move out. Who knows? But I couldn't blame him — if the situation was reversed, I'd be damned if I would have cleaned up spotted sheets for someone else.

His tirade caught me off guard, but I didn't reply. After all, Larry was my favorite bartender. He had introduced me to more women than any other person in Aspen. He had been a Youth Director at a Baptist church in Friendswood, Texas, a small town east of NASA. He had his own baggage. He ran off with one of his flock, Ronda. That was how he came to live in Aspen, a place where his — and my — conduct was not only common, but expected.

It was 1975. Time had passed quickly. I had lived there nearly three years now, but it seemed just a day or two since I had arrived. Aspen was my home. Life there was like a comfortable jacket — warm, welcoming and cozy. Just the thought of leaving my friends left a hole in my soul. Yet, deep down, I knew Larry was right. It was not a town where one could settle. Aspen was a happening — a Woodstock — a perfect escape for young adults to sow their "wild oats." It sure wasn't a place for an adult with a family. When I think back on it, I feel empty and homesick.

The end of the spring ski season ground to an end. Mud and slush filled the streets. The town was empty. All the beautiful tourists returned to their frenzied careers, not to return until next year. I missed my family more than ever. I knew I couldn't return to them, but I could get closer than Aspen and everything it represented to us.

I recklessly loaded all of my belongings into my Audi and headed south. I didn't even take the time to tell my friends goodbye. "Fuck the shop," I thought. "Let dad and doc close it down. I am gone — for good."

Starting Over in Dallas

In July, 1975 I arrived at my brother's home in Garland, Texas. I didn't need to tell him how broke I was. He invited me to stay with him and his family until I could find a job. He worked second shift for a Halliburton Company in Carrolton. His wife worked as a payroll clerk in Richardson. Their two daughters attended day care. About all I could do was cook for them. They could have used some groceries, but I couldn't even afford a loaf of bread.

From the life of Riley; living in luxury, to sleeping on the floor in a vacant bedroom without a dollar to my name, all within thirty days. I felt like a yo-yo — rigged to perpetually spin at the end of the string — twisting around in circles.

One summer's evening, I was sitting around the house with my brother's family, drinking martinis. He called me from work. "Hey, bro, they have a job opening out here in production control. Come on out for an interview. I already spoke with the man doing the hiring. He works nights. Come in the side door marked employees only."

"Well, I would but I have been drinking all evening. Could I come tomorrow?"

"The job will be gone by then."

"What are they going to say about me coming in for an interview smelling like a gin mill?"

"Shit, everyone drinks. If you want to go to work, get your ass out here — tonight!"

I spruced up to the best of my ability. All my clothes were from Aspen. I looked a bit out of place wearing mountain clothes in the summer. I arrived about an hour later. I stopped along the way and picked up a bottle of mouthwash, which I gargled while driving.

I went to the side door, just as he told me. The place was huge. It was probably the largest plant under one roof in Dallas. A fellow caught me gawking around and approached me. "Can I help you?" he said.

"I'm looking for my brother, Roger."

"Where does he work?"

"He's a machinist", I told him.

"We have 250 machine tools here. Can you tell me the department?"

"I don't know. He told me to come out and speak with a guy by the name of Earl. He works in Production Control."

"I know where that is," he said. "Just walk down this aisle until you see an office area. It's the only office in the plant."

I was apprehensive as hell — thinking along the way that maybe I was staggering. After a long walk, I saw the office. I huffed up my chest and strolled in the office.

"Is Earl here?" I asked.

"Just a minute. I'll get him. May I tell him what this is in reference to?"

"My brother told me he had a job opening."

"You are supposed to go through Personnel first," he told me.

"My brother told me he wanted to speak with me before I went to Personnel."

The individual called out over the speaker, "Earl, you have a visitor."

Shortly, a man of small stature walked in. He looked very timid. After salutations, he asked me:

"Ever driven a forklift before?"

"I have driven everything on the planet. I drove my first when I was old enough to see over the wheel."

"This is a bit different," he said. "It has three wheels and can turn on a dime. You drive it backwards while standing up."

"You got one? I'll show you."

"Not tonight," he said. "Come back tomorrow while the sun is still up. We'll see." Guess he smelled the alcohol on my breath.

Of course, I agreed. "See you tomorrow."

He bid me farewell and sent me on my way. Never did he mention anything about Personnel.

My brother spotted me and asked me how it went.

"I think it went well."

"When do you start?"

"He didn't say. He just told me I had to take a test tomorrow."

"What type of test?"

"I have to drive a fork lift."

"Ah, hell. That's a shoe-in. You've been driving since you were in grade school."

"That's what I told him. But he said this was a bit different. He said the tractor only had three wheels on it. I am guessing it's like a John Deere three-wheeler."

"All right. See you when I get off."

Earl said, "Oh, did I tell you the job is on the third shift? The hours are 11:00 p.m. to 7:00 a.m. Can you work those hours?"

"Sure. That would be perfect for me. The house is empty during the day. I can sleep days and work nights. That would be perfect."

Blue Collar Again

I had a very restless night. A bit apprehensive and a lot anxious. Next day I sat around thinking about the test. I was glad when 4:00 p.m. came around, but I had to fight my way through the fifteen miles of rush hour on I-635. What a shocker that was. Dallas was a far cry from the slow pace of Aspen.

I arrived a few minutes late and went straight to Earl's office. He spotted me and asked:

"Are you ready?"

"You bet. Where's the tractor?"

He walked me out to a large concrete pad in the back of the plant. The pad was about 36 inches above the ground.

Pointing to an idle forklift, he said, "There it is. Drive it around about thirty minutes, then I'll come back to observe you. If you can drive it, you've got the job."

I looked at the lift truck, as he called it, and then back to him.

"I told you it was a bit different from a tractor," he said. "Get on it and take off."

I jumped on the thing. "Where's reverse?" I asked.

He showed me, and then walked off.

I figured out where the forward pedal was. There was no gearshift — just a pedal for forward, reverse and speed. I took off and, before I knew it, the thing was traveling at warp speed. The closer I got to the edge of the concrete pad, the more panicky I became.

"Where the shit is the brake? There is no brake! How am I supposed to stop?"

I turned the wheel sharply to avoid running off. The machine turned on a dime all right. The truck listed to the right — so did I. I thought for sure it was going to roll over, but it straightened itself out and I took my foot off the pedal. To my surprise, it stopped abruptly. I stood there, shaking like a dog shitting razor blades. I looked at the rubber marks the tires had left on the concrete. I seriously thought about getting off the damn thing and rushing to my car. It dawned on me that Earl knew all along I was shitting him about being able to drive anything. Earl was probably hiding somewhere, watching me.

Nervously, I tried to move forward again. The rig shot backwards like a crawfish. This time I took my foot off the pedal. Sure enough, it stopped in its tracks. I pressed the pedal forward and, I'll be damned, it went forward. I tried this several times. Then I decided to go in a circle again, but this time with a bit more control. After about thirty minutes of this shit, the whole pad was covered in black skid marks. "Oh well, I tried," I thought to myself.

I saw Earl coming toward me. I stopped the rig and jumped off afraid I would slip and run over him.

"What do you think?" he asked.

"You were right. It's a bit different from what I have driven. But I think I got the general feel for it."

"Okay. When can you start?" he asked.

"How about tomorrow?"

"Not so quick! You still have to go through Personnel. They'll send you out for a physical. If you pass, you'll have to give them your life story, and all the bullshit that goes along with it."

The following Monday, I went to work — $3.00 per hour plus a $.25 per hour premium for working the third shift. It was a shit job for a college graduate, but I was elated just the same. Kind of like chasing a woman — it's not so much the sex as it is the pursuit.

Time flew by. Before I knew it, my ninety-day probation was over. "I can't believe I made ninety days without running into a machine or killing someone," I said to myself. As usual, I had befriended all my co-workers and most of my superiors. Earl called me in for my ninety-day review and said,

"Well, how you do like it?"

I didn't have to lie about it. "It's fantastic," I told him. "Greatest job I ever held."

"You're hired full time then," he said. "Get back to work."

My brother and I celebrated by going to a local hangout that weekend. He introduced me to some of his friends, and they were all friendly towards me. I had a sense of belonging. It was a blast. I could feel the pink cloud forming again. Along with passing my probation period, I also received a small pay increase.

I volunteered for every hour of overtime I could get. I was making enough to find a small apartment. Finally, I moved into my own place. Not that I didn't like living at my brother's, but I felt a bit uncomfortable living there and not paying part of the expenses.

Work was going well. In a couple of months, they promoted me to Expeditor — they even moved me to the second shift. No more forklifts. I had an office job.

I caught on fast. My superiors were more than impressed with my work ethic and my thoroughness. Shortly thereafter, I received another advancement and a commensurate pay increase to go along with it.

Back in the Saddle

I had a couple of girlfriends now — one was married with three lovely children. She was an adopted child and still felt sort of like a reject. She wanted all the adult love she could get — and I, as usual, was more than willing to oblige. Having a wonderful family was not enough for her. After work, we would sit in the parking lot drinking wine until the sun came up. As our relationship developed, we began gathering with other friends and drinking at my apartment.

Yeah, I fell right back into my old routine, fucking everything I set my sights on. She just happened to be the first. For a woman who had given birth to three children, she was a great lay. Even though we never had a relationship beyond sex, we continued to be friends over the next five years.

I enjoyed returning to Aspen occasionally to see my old friends. I would make a weekend trip of it. Sometimes I would take along someone to help me drive. My last visit as an Aspenite, I took Mike, a friend of mine from UT. As soon as I arrived, I called a couple of girlfriends and invited them over. Prior to dinner, one of them came to my house, which I was still paying for. Dawn was a housekeeper for Keith Hefner. She had taught me more than one lesson about sex. One of her specialties was to wait until I was just about to have my orgasm, then flip me over on my back and fuck the shit out of me. We sent Mike to the store for some beer while we caught up on our sex. She was just as good as ever.

That evening we met my other girl-friend Luki, at Don Giovanni's. Luki Seymour was one of my dearest friends. She told me one morning that she slept on my sofa the previous night. She had gone to a party on the hill that turned sour. No one in Aspen locked their doors, so she knew she could walk in at any time. As usual, I came in drunk and walked right past her on my way to bed, never noticing her. We never had sex, but I always fantasized about it. She had no idea how close she came to being another of my concubines. During the course of dinner,

Luki excused herself, said "Good to see you again," and left. Mike ran out the door after her.

"Ray, she was crying. What did you do to her?"

"She hit a guard post in the parking lot and then got stuck. She is upset about something." It was a wild tale, but I had to tell him something.

I knew why she was upset. When I invited her to dinner, I didn't tell her about Dawn and Mike being there. She thought we'd be alone. It never crossed my mind that she might be in love with me. What irony; I'd loved her from the first time I met her, some four years ago. I never thought she would go out with me, so I never asked.

For some reason, it took years for me to realize she was as much in love with me as I was with her. My loss. I just could never bring myself to fuck someone I cared so much about. We met again many years after that. She had become a private physical fitness trainer at the Aspen Athletic Club. Luki was no longer the petite charmer I had remembered. Her body was pumped, ripped from exercise. She had gained thirty pounds — all muscle. Her physique was a dramatic contrast to the pretty little girl I remembered. I didn't know her anymore. She had moved on.

Once a year I went skiing. Sometimes in Aspen. Sometimes in Telluride. On one such trip a group of us went, including Sandy, a very beautiful single mother who worked at the same company I did. We took two vans. One was filled with adults, children and equipment. Sandy and her child rode with me. Her son slept in the rear seat, leaving the two of us to mentally rape each other.

The group stopped in Colorado Springs for breakfast. Afterwards, we laid out our plans for the remainder of the trip. We agreed to stop near Leadville for lunch. Sandy and her son would transfer to the van with her friends for the drive on into Breckenridge. Breckenridge is a small ski resort village. The skiing is good, but the social life sucks.

I knew some short cuts, so I suggested to Sandy that we stop at the Royal Gorge so her son could walk across the bridge. The others went on ahead. I knew I could be at the designated rendezvous at the prearranged time.

Sandy fell asleep after breakfast. I couldn't keep my eyes off her crotch. However, I was very leary about accosting her. I now worked in the personnel office. Any improprieties could get me fired and get the company sued for sexual harassment.

Come sunrise, the wildlife began grazing. Deer and antelope were everywhere. The sun was painting the mountains in hues of burnt orange. God had outdone Himself — again. Sandy and her son were speechless — so was I.

Although the Royal Gorge Park is closed during the winter, visitors can still walk across the bridge, which we did. That bridge scares the hell out of me each time I cross it. The slightest breeze causes it to sway in an exaggerated way. When the park is open, cars can drive across it. Cars really cause it to dance. Today was no different. It had a gentle sway to it. We walked across, stopping occasionally to peer over the side at the river far below. It made my stomach flip. My guests adored it. I loved the fact that they loved it. I was so thankful I didn't fuck that little boy's mother the previous night.

Just down the road from the Royal Gorge, we turned north on a dirt road. The road stretched across one ranch — no fences, just a couple of cattle guards. It's a fifty mile trip — one damn big ranch. Sandy looked a bit concerned at first. Then she settled in and let her guard down. We talked about nothing for the rest of the trip into Leadville. The three of us just admired the beautiful landscape.

When we arrived, the other people were waiting. We joined them for lunch. She brought them up to date on everything we had seen and done. They were envious. Who wouldn't be? My ego was so over-inflated; it felt like the Goodyear blimp.

After lunch, I told Sandy she could reach me in Aspen by calling my friend, Steve. She was to call when they got ready to return to Dallas. Unfortunately, Steve had a change of telephone listings. For over a decade, he had only listed his first name in the telephone directory. Everyone knew him. That was the way I instructed Sandy to contact me. "Just call information for STEVE. I'll be there. Leave a message."

Unbeknownst to me, Steve had loaned his home to an executive from MCA Records. I had no idea he had out of town guests. I bathed and lay down for a "short" nap before spending the night on the town. My nap turned into a 20-hour deep sleep.

The next morning the phone rang, and I jumped up to answer. It was for the MCA executive. He was standing in the kitchen and he let me know in no uncertain terms that I was an uninvited guest to their weekend of privacy.

"Ah. You must be the fellow from Oklahoma. We enjoyed listening to you snore all night. You made for good entertainment. We sat around the sofa and tapped our toes to your raucous snoring." What a bunch of jerks. Why didn't they just wake me up? I was both embarrassed and pissed.

I left Aspen and headed to Breckenridge in the hopes of meeting up with the rest of the group. I managed to find my fellow travelers' vehicle, but no sign of them. I left a note on their windshield informing them I was going to a different resort and finished it with, "I'll see you back in Dallas."

I figured, screw the other resort. I didn't have the money to stay at any lodge. I had chosen Aspen over Brackenridge because I knew I could stay at Steve's free. With that option gone, off to Dallas I went.

When Sandy returned to work, she came stalking into my office. "I tried to call you. They had no listing for a "STEVE" in the phone book. I got tired of the group and wanted come stay with you the rest of the week."

"Damn," I thought. "Another piece of ass lost." Nonetheless, I was impressed she wanted to come and stay with me. She was one hot momma. "It simply was not meant to be," I thought.

Ski Bum

Heading into winter of '75, one of my male friends at work introduced me to a petite twenty-one-year-old, black haired, brown eyed, Mexican-American beauty. Terri was an innocent child. Very timid, but willing to be laid just the same. Peer pressure might have had something to do with that. The first time we made love, I took her to Lake Way on Lake Travis, near Austin. We purchased a case of beer before leaving Dallas and drank half of it before we got there. We were both apprehensive about our impending fling in bed. She had good reason. Her first sexual encounter was with a Dallas police officer. He used a condom.

"He hurt me" she confided. "Are you going to use one?" she asked.

"No. I didn't bring any with me."

She relaxed somewhat after that. I couldn't get enough of her; we had sex four times that night. At last she had an orgasm; it was her first. I was impressed. I was the second man to have sex with her and the first to give her an orgasm. She opened her heart to me after that. For the first time, I was in love with a woman I was sleeping with — outside of marriage that is.

The next morning while walking the shoreline of the lake, she told me, "I was about to get mad at you. You wouldn't leave me alone. Every time I'd get to sleep, you were back on top of me."

She was right. I couldn't get enough of her. I could sense it in her eyes and tone of voice — she was in love. As was I.

Our trip back to Dallas was much more relaxed than the trip to the motel. All apprehension was gone, and we spoke candidly about living together. That day, she came to my place after work. She had a small tote bag, containing a change of clothes. I was pleasantly shocked. Finally, I had found the love of my life.

Over the next six months, we made love every minute we were together — stopping only long enough to eat and get a drink. At one point, she asked, "Do you wear a condom? Are you coming inside me?" That was not like her. She didn't know what the word "come" meant when we first had sex. Now she was speaking openly about it. She'd obviously been talking to some friend about our relationship and the countless times we had had sex. Moreover, she was wondering why she had not gotten pregnant. This had crossed my mind as well. As much as I loved her, I wouldn't have cared. I could have spent a lifetime with her.

Joy, love and merriment best defined our relationship. We treasured each moment together. Terri was such a sweet girl. She was the light of my life.

An old sailor once told me, "If you want to get rid of your spouse, just take them on a one-month trip on a small boat." Long before the voyage ends, one or the other will want a divorce — long before you reach land. The same goes with skiing with a non-skier. Like an idiot, I took her skiing.

By March, Terri and I had become such a team I thought it was time to take her with me. By no means was I an expert skier, but I had taught a few how to snowplow. I figured Terri was a fast learner. She'd catch on. There was not a lot of discretionary income between us. I had a couple pairs of old Levis tailored to fit her. We discussed the trip at some length. A married couple who worked at the same company I did told me of their plans to go to Telluride. Both held full time jobs at the company and were full-time students as well. The plan was to meet up with some fellow employees who lived in Denver, but had never skied. They needed someone to share the cost of the trip. It was a perfect opportunity to take Terri.

We set out in their van. Terri and I occupied the rear seat, occasionally slipping into the rear of the van to sleep and cuddle. We ate weed-laced brownies along the way. There was not much sobriety during the long, grueling trip. Having been to Telluride on previous ski trips, I found some rooms at a small ski dormitory which had once served as a church. The "great room" on the ground floor was wall-to-wall with throw pillows and cushy sofas and chairs. A huge fireplace crackled in the background. Quite romantic!

We walked across the street to a grocery store and picked up some staples, after which we retired for the evening. The setting was conducive for snuggling, but drinking was out, at least for the first day. Every time I had been in Telluride, it took two days to acclimatise to the altitude. Next day, we were off to the mountain for a much-anticipated day of skiing. I took the non-skiers on the "T" lift and taught them the basics. By noon, most were skiing well enough that they were not going to kill themselves, or others. That was MOST. Terri was the one exception. I finally coaxed her to go to the top with me. I could tell by the look on her face that she was scared shitless.

"She'll adjust after a few trips down the slope," I thought. I'd had the same fear when I first hit the slopes.

She scooted off the chair without incident. Dismounting from the chair and retaining one's balance is often the most troublesome part of skiing, so I figured everything was okay. Then Terri looked down toward the road. Bad mistake! The cars looked like little ants scurrying back to their den. People were just specks. Her face was ashen white.

"Terri, six of my co-workers are skiing today for their first time. We're supposed to meet up with them at the base to see how they're progressing and to have a bite to eat. If they can do it, so can you."

Terri was silent. Her breathing labored, her face a mask of fear, she looked like she was on the verge of bursting into tears. We made a very slow approach toward the most gentle of the slopes. She did okay with her snowplowing. Twenty yards later, her knees began trembling. God knows, she was about the most pathetic-looking child I had ever seen.

I gave her time to regain her composure. We tried another ten-yard run. I reached out and held her hand. She was quivering all over by now.

"Honey, don't think about it. Don't look any further down than the next twenty feet."

Again, total silence. She looked at me with those puppy-dog eyes as if to say, "Please don't throw me off the bridge". Before we could even ski the next ten yards, she fell. I tried everything I knew to coax her. She lay in the snow crying. Frustrated by this time, I suggested I ski on down and see how the others were doing, giving her time to acclimatise. I promised to catch the next lift up.

When I got back from my rendezvous with the others, I skied to where I had left her. I found this poor little frightened girl scooting down the mountain on her butt. Skis in one hand, and snow in the other!

"What have I done?" I stopped beside her. She was whimpering, tears streaming down her raspberry-tinted cheeks.

"If she's trying to make me feel sorry for her, she certainly has succeeded," I thought. Seeing her in such distress pained me. But I had other commitments too. It was time to meet up with my other skiers on the bunny trail.

"I hate to leave you by yourself babe, but I promised the others we would meet them at the base. Let me go down and tell them we are having some issues. You stay here and look around. I'll be back within an hour and walk you down."

To Terri, walking down the slope was just as frightening as skiing. She was terrified of heights. Standing on the side of that mountain must have been as scary for her as it would have been for me to stand atop a 60-story structure with nothing but red-iron beams to walk on. My hindsight is painfully perfect.

Downhill Slide

When I finally caught up the other members it was just past lunch. They were having a blast and no one had been injured — yet. I went back to the top to look for my love, but she was nowhere to be found! My heart sank. I was both remorseful and fear-struck. I worked my way down the mountain, searching the out-of-bounds areas, hoping to find her in one piece.

"Maybe she built up the courage to go ahead on her own. Maybe someone took pity on her and helped her down. I'll go to the lodge. If she's not up here, that's where she will be. We can get a cup of hot chocolate and a cinnamon roll. That will do us both good."

The committee inside my head was chattering so loud, I couldn't concentrate. About two-thirds of the way down, I saw a ski patrolman loading someone into his rescue toboggan. This happens frequently on beginner's slopes. Beginners sprain their ankles when first learning. Or they pretend to be injured just to get a free trip down in a basket. As I got closer, I saw it was Terri. She was the victim.

"Oh shit. She's hurt. Here we are in Telluride, no money and she's hurt."

I slid up to the two as he was strapping her in.

"Are you her mate?" the patrolman asked

"Yes. Is she OK?"

"Don't you ever leave a beginner stranded on the slopes! You could have alerted us and we would have rescued her within minutes. That is heartless. Take her skis. I'll tow her down."

I felt like someone had caught me sodomizing a baby kitten. He was right. "What kind of an asshole would run off and leave a friend alone on a strange mountain?" I thought to myself.

Shame blanketed me. What had I done? That was so unlike me. Were the other six beginners more important to me than Terri? My quest for ego fulfillment took precedence over Terri. The incident played repeatedly in my head the rest of the day — and beyond.

Terri spent the rest of the day in the lodge. At day's end, we returned her skis and headed in town to get a beer. Although she looked a little better, she was deeply hurt. Her only friend in this strange place had walked away from her in a time of great need.

We made up overnight. Next morning I thought we would have breakfast in a nearby restaurant and head for the slopes.

"I'll leave you some money for drinks and food. You can stay at the base lodge and bask in the sun," I said.

"I'm not going."

"Terri, I am so sorry for yesterday. I wasn't thinking. What I did was heartless. Please come with me — I'll stop every trip down to see you."

"You go on. I'll tour the town. I need to pick up some souvenirs anyhow."

"Please, babe, come with me."

"No."

The way she said "no" made it quite clear that not all the pleading in the world was going to get her back on the slope. We were to return to Dallas the next day.

"I'll be damned if I am going to miss a day of skiing just to please her," I said to myself.

The rest of us had an extraordinary day, skiing, drinking and smoking a little weed on the lift. The novice skiers were good for my ego. They each had to show me what they had learned. Their progress was impressive indeed. All thoughts of Terri were muted with pride, ego, merriment, and, of course, a concoction of mind altering substances.

By the time we got back to the dormitory, we were beginning to feel the effect of the altitude and the wear and tear on our knees. We went directly to the dorm to change clothes and get a beer. I walked in expecting Terri to be in front of the fireplace, or in our room. As I turned to go upstairs, Terri called out, "We are in here, Ray."

I turned around to see her sitting in a small room with two men from Dallas. They had spent the day smoking dope. My heart sank. The scene was one straight out of a dime novel. As blood rushed to my head, I felt faint. "Have they been high all day? They probably fucked all day." Ditch weed has that affect. Sort of like drinking, only more effective in reducing one's inhibitions.

I couldn't bring myself to look her in the eyes, let alone speak to her. I returned to the room and began packing. I didn't feel like going out with our friends to drink suds and swap lies about how great a day we'd had. It was a low point of my life — I was crushed. I was accustomed to breaking others' hearts. Now it was my heart that was aching.

I packed my things into the back of the van and crawled in. The van was filled with pillows and down quilts. I just wanted to sulk. Within half an hour, Terri came with her things. The silence was deafening.

"Aren't you going to come in and join the rest of us?"

"No. I don't think I will. Tell them goodbye for me."

The grueling trip back to Dallas was solemn. Terri and I didn't talk. The other couple repeatedly asked if I was okay — they didn't know about Terri's day with the boys. "Yeah. I'm fine. Just worn out." They knew better. My body language told another story — and it put a damper on the party. I had rained on everyone's parade.

We got to Dallas late the next evening. I had a lot to think about, so I went on to bed. Terri came in to lie down with me. I rolled over to show my disapproval, and she cried softly. I wasn't supposed to hear it. It was all I could do to keep from wrapping my arms around her warm body and reassuring her that everything would work out, but by then I had pretty well made up my mind to move to another apartment and leave her there. My two children were to spend their summer with me that year. Originally, I had hoped Terri would stay with us. God knows, I could have used her help with the children.

I found an apartment near work. Terri knew she was not welcome. Poor child. She had done nothing wrong other than spending the day with the boys. She had broken my heart. And I hers. Like two wounded animals, we each went our own way. Alas, the Karma Cop had caught up with me!

As was always the case, everything worked out for the children and me. I found a live-in nanny. She cooked and cared for the kids, and they kept me busy all summer. Gradually, I forgot about the pain deep within my heart, and about Terri altogether.

Country Clubbing

By Spring of 1977, I had received several promotions at work. I had just enough discretionary income to join the county club and the kids and I went there often to swim and play. I still couldn't afford the meals at the club though, so we got by on snacks and soft drinks.

Summer passed all too rapidly. The kids returned to Austin in early August. The apartment felt empty. My attention quickly turned to my neighbors. One, Donna, was about twenty-two. She was a divorcee with two small children. The other was a seventeen-year-old inside the body of a twenty-something. It was not long before the mania returned. I was burning the candle at both ends. I had lived with it so long, it seemed like an old friend; it had served me well in the past, in an insane sort of way.

I wasted no time in developing my relationships with the two neighbors. I trained Donna to wake me up in the morning and brew my coffee. Now she had three kids to look after — her two and me. I gave her a key so she could let herself in. She couldn't just knock on the door and run off. Now she had to come to my bed. This worked great for me. When I heard her fiddling with the door lock, I'd get aroused. By the time she was in my room, I was ready for a little roll in the hay. She was not all that crazy about being pulled into bed each morning but, then again, she didn't complain either.

Each day began with Donna and ended with Kari (not my ex). Kari had a rich boyfriend, an heir to the Phillip's estate - a hell of a nice young man, for a rich kid. She and I went to the country club one Sunday for some sun and a bit of foreplay in the pool. About mid-afternoon, a rather handsome young man strolled up and grabbed Kari around the waist.

"Who the shit does he think he is?" I thought.

"Ray, this is my boyfriend, Carl. Carl, this is my neighbor I told you about."

"Pleased to meet you, Ray. What do you do?"

"You mean for a living?"

"Yes. For a living."

"I'm a recruiter for Halliburton. What do you do, Carl?"

"Nothing. Mostly play."

"Well shit, here is another frickin' trust fund freak," I thought.

It was a bit humbling, playing second fiddle to Carl. Kari and I continued having our evening flings, but by day she belonged to Carl. Kari's mom encouraged our relationship, even though I was thirteen years Kari's senior. Mom would invite me to Sunday lunch, and everything would be normal. Let mom invite Carl, and Kari was all over him. I got the message — I was okay in a pinch (in the dark).

Donna also kept a lover in the closet. They had dated for two years. He only came around when he was horny. I was his surrogate. It hurt my feelings a bit but, then again, it made it easier for me to play the field. There was just something about making a commitment that I abhorred. Women seem to like the idea of keeping a significant other in the wings at all times. I, on the other hand, was an opportunist, preferring to take advantage of the moment.

One evening, there was a knock on my door. "Ray, I'm Buzz, a friend of Donna's. A gal we know is having a party at her house this evening. Would you like to come? Donna and I are going. There will be plenty of booze. Annie keeps her fridge stocked."

"Any single women going?" I asked.

"Well, Annie is single. She's a widow. Her husband died a year ago. My brother and I were both friends of Dean and Annie."

"Sure she won't mind?"

"Absolutely not. Donna told me you were single. I told Annie. Now she wants to meet you. It's my birthday! I'd be honored to have you."

"What time Buzz?"

"Let's make it around seven-ish."

"You're on."

I dashed about, laying out just the right casual clothes. There was no time to go shopping for a birthday gift. However, I did have a half bag of weed in my car. I put a ribbon on it and stuck it in my pocket.

After a day of martinis, I was one leg up on the drinking. I pulled up to a rather large home in an upper-middle class neighborhood. Mother had bought a new car and given me her two-year-old Cadillac. It was a beauty, all black inside and out. "Glad I brought the Caddy," I thought. As if I was accustomed to such homes, I strolled to the front door with my chest leading the way. Annie answered the door.

"Hello. I'm Ray. Buzz invited me to a party here. Am I at the right address?"

"You are. We were expecting you."

Wow! This was a classy woman. Tall, slender, a bit flat-chested and very well manicured. A very striking woman indeed. I was in heat — again. Annie had two adolescent children, Jeff and Lori. Both were well mannered but a bit aloof, I thought.

People began singing "Happy Birthday" and thrusting gifts towards Buzz, anxiously waiting for him to open them. But I had no gift to give him — in public, leastwise. I felt like an outsider. "Discretion. Discretion," I told myself as I waited my turn to give him his gift.

At last, I caught him alone and handed him the small plastic bag, with the bow taped to the side. He gave me this blank look, but thanked me just the same. Now I did feel awkward.

We drank, partied, played parlor games and danced to the music of the '70s. What a great time. I finally got a chance to dance with Annie. She had the prettiest brown eyes. A real standout. One dance led to another — then another. Finally, we turned off the music and retired to the solarium to drink and talk. Annie kept close to me. My heart pounded as I fantasized about all the possibilities.

When it was time to break up and go home, I thanked Annie and bid her farewell.

"Annie, I belong to a country club. Any chance you and the children could have dinner with me some evening?"

"Sure. I would enjoy that and I know the children would like getting out of the house. Let me give you my number. Call me when you would like to go."

"Oh my gosh!" I thought. "She likes me."

I could hardly wait until the next day to call and set a date. She sounded excited to hear from me. When the day rolled around, she, the kids, and I headed to the club. The kids had all sort of questions:

"Do you have any children?"

"Yes, two. A little boy going on seven. His name is Steven. And a daughter, five. Her name is Krisi."

"Where do you work, Mr. Tune?"

"Halliburton, in Carrollton."

"What do you do there?"

"I work in personnel. I recruit and hire people for the shop."

"That's enough questions, kids. Give Ray a rest."

Jeff, Annie's son, was rather tall for his age. He was not athletic, but strong just the same. He was a bit shy, but for a boy of fourteen, he had been through a lot. Lori, on the other hand, was quite vivacious after she got to know you — she chattered all the time. She was precocious and very flirty. She, like her brother, Jeff, was fairly tall and quite slim — not skinny, just trim. She was two years younger than Jeff and a bit of a fireball. Her left eyelid drooped a bit, looking like it was in deep sleep. Lori was born with scoliosis. I suspect that had something to do with her eye. The children attended a private church school. Both were well mannered, always respectful of their mother.

We pulled up in front of the club and handed the keys to the valet. He escorted us to the restaurant, and then returned to our car. With that Cadillac, I could get into any club. It was intimidating, to say the least. We chatted, exchanged barbs, giggled and feasted until we were bloated.

"We'd better get home, Ray. Thanks for a wonderful dinner."

"It was great. I enjoyed the family setting. It's been a long time for me. Do you want to do it again sometime?"

"Sure. Why don't you come have dinner with us Saturday evening?"

"I'd love that. What time?"

"Come over about five. We can have a few drinks. Dinner will be ready around six."

"I'm looking forward to it."

I felt like I had hit the big leagues. She was the most cultured woman I ever dated. She became bolder and a bit more demanding of my time. By then, Terri was history — she hadn't entered my mind. But when Donna told Annie about our morning meetings, she thought that was a bit too cozy.

Only three months after we first met, sometime during the winter, Annie asked me, "Would you like to move in with us?"

I was elated. "Are you sure?" I asked.

"The children love you and so do I. Well?"

"I'd love that." I replied.

"I'll help you move. Buzz has a pickup. We can pack the heavier things on it."

"I don't want to impose on him. But I might want to use his truck."

"He thinks you're the cat's meow. Ever since you gave him the baggie, he has been talking about you. At first, he was alarmed. He asked me how I knew he smoked weed. He was really paranoid until I told him that the weed was the only gift you had to give him."

Two weeks later Annie began hounding me to make the move. I was ready. This was my grand opportunity to make a fresh start in my life. I thought; let the past remain in the past. It would be different this time. There were no cash problems. I had a beautiful woman and a ready-made family. She was a terrific cook and housekeeper. How could I possibly screw this one up?

"Perhaps the insanity will go into remission," I prayed. It seemed like I was on a perpetual high.

Market Madness

I was well into my graduate program for the second time. I worked diligently at both work and school. The hard work was paying off. I had received five promotions within four years. My ego was re-inflated. I was so puffed up I couldn't see my feet. The harder I worked, the more I drank. Just as Buzz had told me, Annie kept the liquor cabinet full at all times.

My brother-in-law, Jimmy, taught me the ins-and-outs of commodity trading. Jimmy and my sister had been married about ten years. He and I got along great. Annie and I worked together on our research — sometimes working until two in the morning. She was an extremely bright woman, with an IQ of 138. With her intelligence and my education we were ready to hit the big time.

We made $500 on our first trade. We hadn't even sent our margin money in yet. Using Jimmy's advice, we built our cash balance up to $20,000. Rather than pay taxes on our unexpected gain(s), we opened trading accounts for our friends. One such friend was my ex-wife, Kari. We made enough money in her account, in one month, to prepay child support for both children until they turned eighteen. We made $5,000 for a casual friend who worked as a firefighter in Dallas.

Annie and I thought we needed a farm as well. Hell, we were aristocrats. One can't be an aristocrat without a country estate. Investment bankers came to our house with the newest "get rich" schemes. Our heads were spinning with success. My ego became unruly — orbiting somewhere around Mars.

Towards the end of our commodity marathon, we became a bit sloppy. We took our streak of luck for granted. Then it toppled, like the straw house it was. One afternoon, I was in a conference at the Holiday Inn. A concierge interrupted the meeting to inform me I had a phone call. I took the call expecting that someone had had a heart attack, or been in a wreck. It was much worse. It was my brother-in-law.

"Get out of the market now! It's about to crash." He hung up.

I couldn't think. "What the shit am I supposed to do? Call the broker . . . call the broker," I thought. I called my private number in the broker's office (yeah, it was a "red" phone). My hands were trembling so much I could barely hold the phone.

"Dump everything at current prices. Do it now while I am on the phone!"

Within a couple of minutes, he said, "It's a done deal. How did you know the market was going to crash?"

"I didn't. It was just a hunch."

I know he didn't believe me. Within twenty minutes, the market was down ninety points. Due to the fact that the market had closed limit-up for three consecutive days, the Commodity Exchange removed the limits, allowing the market to move as much as the traders wanted. If I'd had the presence of mind, not only would I have closed all my open positions, I would have sold the market short. A short sale would have made more money for us in thirty minutes than we had made on all the previous trades combined. Annie and I were content to get out with what gains we had. After all, child support was prepaid for life, we owned a farm, bought a new Audi, a 1.5-carat marquise diamond wedding ring, and still had $20,000 in our trade account.

I slid down that same old slope I had traversed so many times in the past. Drinking had become the norm. Between classes at college, my fellow graduate students and I would drink a quart of Bloody Marys. After class, we'd drink some more. Night after night, I came home drunk, not knowing how I had made it.

At times, I didn't even remember the trip. I came home one night on two rims. I didn't even realize it until the next morning when I got ready to go to work. "Damn. Someone cut my tires last night! Mean sons-of-bitches. If I catch them, I'll yank their fucking heads off." The voices in my head had already tried and convicted the perpetrators. But as I moved closer to the car I saw I had obviously hit something or someone on my way home. They weren't cut.

The rims were worn down to the hub on the wheel. I had run the tires off the rims.

"Oh shit, I wonder if I got a ticket. Man, I have got to stop driving when I am drunk. I'm going to get caught. If I lose my license, I'm screwed. I can't afford for this to get back to Helen." Helen was my supervisor at work. Annie and I kept silent about it and told the children not to say a word.

Night Terror

Annie and I decided a camping trip to the farm would bring me down a rung or two. We loaded a tent and other camping equipment into an old 1951 Chevy pickup I had purchased from the Richardson Public School District. It was mid-October. The temperature was in the seventies. We had sweat running down the cracks of our butts from setting up the tent and equipment.

After the rigors of setting up camp, Annie cooked a wonderful meal. She was right. This was so peaceful I couldn't have behaved badly even if I had wanted to. The meal demanded a round of wine. Then another, and another, until Annie and I were shitfaced. The lot of us turned in for the night. About midnight, it became eerily quiet. No screech owls. No crickets or cicada. Just silence. Then the sound of the wind came whispering through the trees. It got closer and closer. It reminded me of a predator moving in for the kill. Like a bolt of lightning, something started pummeling our tent. I got up to pee and see what was hitting the tent. It was sleeting.

"How could the weather have turned so violent so quickly?" I thought. I pulled on my blue jeans and slipped on the old mudder boots from Aspen. I had no warm outerwear, only a light Levi jacket. I braved the freezing wind and sleet and began gathering firewood. "It may not help much, but it sure will look good," I thought to myself. The gallon of jug wine was still sitting on the hood of the truck. "I'll take a couple of swigs. Might warm me a bit."

I heard twigs breaking near the tent. It was Lori. She probably thought since I was outside, it was safe for her to relieve her bladder. She peed standing up, knees slightly bent, hands on her knees. I grew up on a farm where kids peed in the yard. Girls squatted and boys stood up. Lori pissed like a boy — standing up. I'd never seen this before. As shameful as it might have been, seeing her pee aroused me. "Don't act on it. Don't you dare act on it," I kept telling myself.

I stood motionless near the pickup door, hanging on to my wine bottle. Having satisfied her call of nature, she came to where I was standing. She never said a word — just threw her arms around me and looked me in the eyes. I knew what that look meant — she wanted me. To break the mood, I turned her away from me and pulled her body near mine, to keep her warm. That prevented her from kissing me, but it didn't dampen my carnal thoughts.

"What if I slipped my hand down her pants? What would she do? She might scream and awaken her mom. Then again, she might want to go a little further... NO. DO NOT REACT!"

That was a close call. Finally, the two of us set off in separate directions to gather more wood. The fire was crackling. Sparks began rocketing upwards into the frigid night. The blaze was now huge.

"Let's go to bed. Should be warm enough by now."

She acted as if I had rejected her — which I did. Not willingly. But I did. Her mom slept between the two of us, thank God. I was as addicted to sex as a wino is to wine. Each time I glanced toward her, her little bright eyes were staring at me. At long last, I slipped off into a sound sleep. Later, I asked a friend of mine if peeing while standing was common. She said, "That's a 'Girl Scout thing'".

Next morning, Annie and Jeff went out to make the obligatory bio call.

"Ray, come out and look at this. The tent and truck are coated with sleet or snow."

"I know. I went out last night to build up the fire. It was sleeting hard then."

Lori never uttered a word. I thought she would surely tell them she had also ventured outside. Never a word. This concerned me deeply.

We broke camp and headed back to Dallas. It was quiet all the way back. We snacked on cheese and crackers and kept our mouths closed. I couldn't help but think how close I had come to fingering Little Miss Sunshine. "Why so mum?" I pondered. "Perhaps everyone is tired or, maybe Lori told Annie about our uncomfortable encounter in the midst of the night." Did Annie sense the fondness Lori and I shared for each other?"

My close encounter with Lori haunted me for days. Alcohol seemed to eradicate the memory of her advance. The dark side of my persona was back where it had been in Aspen — maybe even worse.

Lurking Lolita

Christmas of '77, Mother came to visit us. It was great having her. I wanted to show off the lush quarters I now lived in — something she never got to experience for herself. Annie and Mom sat in the kitchen babbling about everything under the sun — mostly me. I stayed in the living room to give them time to get acquainted. As I sat in my favorite lounge chair watching TV, Lori came in and jumped on my lap. My hands were folded on top of my lap. I have a nervous tick — stroking my index fingers over my thumb. My grandfather had the same thing (Grandma called it fiddling). Lori threw her left arm around my neck and bounced around on my lap. Suddenly, she stopped jumping and went into this solemn trance. I removed my hand to scratch my nose. Quick as a flash she grabbed my left hand and thrust it back under her skirt. "Oh-oh! She's at it again," I thought. This little trickster had been working on an orgasm, at my expense

I started to push her off my lap and Jeff bolted through the front door. Without so much as a glance, she hollered, "Mom, Ray is touching my privates."

I was aghast. The little liar was covering her butt.

The women went on chatting, pretending not to have heard her. Beyond a doubt, that was the most humiliating experience of my life. Despite that, we all spent the day eating and catching up on the state of the family.

Annie attended college at night at Richardson community college, twenty miles or so from the house. Lori knew the routine well. One evening, after Annie left for classes, Lori sat on my lap again. She was in her nightgown — nothing unusual for her. She grabbed my hand and again thrust it under her bottom. I remained perfectly still. She looked at me and said, "Well. Aren't you going to do anything?"

"Nope. I am not. Get up."

"Why?"

"Because the last time you broadcast it to the world. Now get off my lap."

"Well, Jeff saw us. I had to say something."

"I was not doing anything Lori."

She was crushed. Another "woman scorned".

Since my NDE, my precognitive abilities had developed to the point that I took them for granted. My kids came up from Austin the following summer. One night I had a feeling that something was amiss. I went to the kids' room. They slept in a room on the other side of the solarium — directly across the room from our bedroom. Instead of going through the solarium, I took the long route through the kitchen.

Jeff had Kris pulled to the end of her bed. He just was standing there. Krisi's panties were off. Instead of going off on Jeff, I said, "Jeff. Get out of here before I get mad. Don't you ever go in their room in the night again."

Jeff looked like a deer in the beam of a high-powered light. He ran out of the room. I tucked Kris in and went by Jeff's room just to satisfy myself that he had actually gone to bed. He had.

Next day, I told Annie about the previous evening. She just looked at me as if to say, "So what?" Her lackadaisical attitude caught me off guard. I expected a little support from her. She was every bit a lady — in all things, at all times — but she was no prude. To her sex was just another bodily function.

Toward the end of the summer, Lori invited a neighbor girl for a sleep-in. During the night, I keep hearing giggling. "Enough is enough," I said to myself. I walked down the long hallway into the family room. The two girls had Steven pinned between them, playing with his genitals.

"Oh, my God," I said to myself.

"Girls, let Steven go to bed. Both of you go to your room and get in bed." Without so much as a look, they got up and returned to Lori's room, giggling along the way.

Next day, I confronted Annie about the children's behavior. "Annie, both the children are predators and opportunists. I caught Jeff messing with Kris about a week ago. Krisi was asleep. Her panties were off. I didn't touch him. However, I did let him know that was unacceptable behavior. Lori groped me Christmas day and tried to blame

me. Last night I found the two girls fondling Steven —
while he was awake. What's wrong with these kids?"

"Dean (her deceased husband) used to demand
that we go naked when inside the house. I guess they got
aroused somewhere along the way. Dean and I never
thought anything about it."

"Did Dean ever molest the children?" I asked.

"Not that I know of," she replied.

Okay, now I understood their aberrant behavior.
"Let it be. Now that it's in the open, they'll stop it," I
rationalized.

Trouble in Paradise

Annie and I argued nightly. It didn't make any difference what the point was. We just argued. If there was nothing to criticize her about, I made up some shit. One night, after an intense argument about the children, I slapped her. That was the beginning of the end. She encouraged me to see a marriage counselor. The one she selected just happened to be a psychiatrist. What a coincidence.

At the end of our first meeting, the doctor said, "Ray, you have what we call a manic-depressive personality. I suggest you begin a regimen of lithium. Take it once a day to begin with." According to him, Annie had no afflictions.

I have to admit, the lithium worked — for a while — but the side effects were a bit too harsh for me. I couldn't think clearly and my speech became discombobulated. This put me at a disadvantage with my fellow students. Our grades were based, in part, on class participation – an extremely competitive exercise. One had to fight to get the floor — which was the desired effect, as I later determined. The professor was teaching us how to be assertive, so he said. I only tried this at work one time — my superiors told me I was abrasive and rude. So I stopped taking the lithium.

Slippery Slope

During Spring break of '78, Annie and I planned a ski trip to Aspen. We booked a room for a week in a condominium. It had been one of my favorite haunts when I lived in Aspen. We took the children with us. "What the hell? I'll teach them to ski. Annie can get private instruction."

Seems I never learn from my previous mistakes. It was only two years ago that I lost Terri as a direct result of trying to give her private ski lessons. One of the fastest ways to get a divorce is to teach your significant other how to ski, or take them on a month-long sailing trip. Either poison works.

Which brings me to another truism a seasoned sailor told me: "No close relationship can exist in a vacuum." He should know; he and his wife sailed from Galveston to St. Croix on their 25-foot sail boat. They divorced within ninety days of their return. He told me each was ready to throw the other overboard by the end of the first week. For a relationship to endure and flourish, a couple must have social intercourse outside the marriage. Didn't work for me, but hey — what did? I was a social butterfly and still couldn't keep a lasting relationship. Maybe it had something to do with keeping my pants on, a skill I hadn't quite mastered.

Two days into our vacation, we walked into the lobby at the condominiums. It had been a rigorous day of playing on the slopes. An ex-neighbor of mine from Laurel Mountain was tending the check-in counter. The minute she spotted me, she yelled:

"Ray! I need to speak with you."

"Hey, I'm surprised to see you. Pleasantly surprised. How have you been?"

"Ray, the Sheriff's department has been trying to reach you all day. Every ski slope had signs up for "Ray" to call them. They called all hotels, motels and condos as well."

"Why are they looking for me? I haven't been here long enough to get into any shit."

"It's your mother, Ray. She had a stroke or something. She's in the Bethany Hospital in Oklahoma City. They don't expect her to live through the night. Your father wants you to return tonight."

Only my father would have known how to find me among the 100,000 people in Aspen on that weekend. My heart sank. Annie, the kids, and I retired to our condo to think about what we were going to do. We called the airport, thinking we could leave the car in Aspen and return later to pick it up, but all flights in and out were suspended due to a blizzard.

"Annie, we are stranded. All flights are canceled for the remainder of the day and probably tomorrow as well. If they can't fly, I don't know how we can possibly drive." Annie and the children were mute — not even a chirp.

But I couldn't wait out the weather. "Pack up. We're going to drive out tonight. I think I know a pass we can drive over, even in this storm. I've never been over it in a car — just my Blazer. My mom and dad once came over Independence Pass when it was blanketed with a foot of snow, in this same car. The snow was up to the bumper. When you grow up in Western Oklahoma, you learn to drive in blizzards."

Annie packed while I went to the City Market to load up on sandwich stuff, drinks, the usual survival foods such as peanut butter and jam, and ten pounds of apples. Upon returning to the Inn, the condo staff had all our belongings set outside, ready to load. We packed everything in the trunk except for the food.

Without so much as a word, we drove off, not knowing what to expect. I am sure Annie and the kids thought I was a certifiable mental case — after all I was putting all of us at risk just so I could tell my family I had done everything possible. My father was very familiar with Colorado blizzards. He would have damn well understood. Be that as it may, for the sake of my ego, I felt compelled to forge ahead in order to prove to my siblings that, by God, nothing could stop me.

The Great Race

We drove through the blizzard, never thinking about how the end goal would turn out. I didn't think about Annie or the children. There wasn't anything or anyone going to stop me.

By the grace of God, we made it to Ruidoso Pass. I made my usual left at Ruidoso to head out across the 100-mile trek towards Hereford, Texas. Just as I turned onto the highway, we ran into a roadblock. Two officers greeted me.

"The road is closed sir. You'll have to go through Tucumcari if you hope to go east."

"Officer, my mother is dying in Oklahoma City. I've got to get through. I've driven this road dozens of times. I know how to drive in the snow."

"We can't allow you to pass. Two travelers had their windshields blown out just up the road. We can't get patrol cars out there. The ambulances can't make it. Sorry, but you have to go around. We recommend you spend the night in Ruidoso. I don't know how you made it this far in this storm. How were the roads from Aspen to here?"

"They're snow packed. Six to eight inches. Wind is steady, but not dangerous."

I was lying through my teeth, but I had to stress the point that I was no ordinary traveler — I was above nature's tirades.

We turned around and headed south toward Tucumcari. Fifty miles down the highway, we were plowing snow with our front bumper. If it hadn't been for some tracks left by an 18-wheeler, I wouldn't have known that I was on the road.

"Ray, how can you see where you are going?" asked Annie.

"I'm just following the tracks, dear. Don't worry."

"What if that truck ran off the road?"

"Annie, that's all I have to guide me." I shrugged and kept going. Sometimes you have to play the hand you're dealt.

Every few miles, I had to get out and clean balls of ice from my windshield wipers. The ball was as large as a five-pound bag of sugar. My head was splitting from watching the whirling torrents of snow as it funneled into my windshield. I had vertigo so bad, I was sick to my stomach. The snowstorm had turned into a whiteout.

Last Call

It was early in the morning when we broke free of the blizzard. We had just crossed the New Mexico-Oklahoma state line. It was still snowing like a bitch, but visibility was a bit better, mostly due to the light of the sun peeking through the snow clouds. I hammered it for the remainder of the trip.

I was groggy, I couldn't think. We stopped several times to fuel up and make bio calls. It was difficult to stand — we had been sitting for so long — and walking was extremely painful. We staggered to and from the restrooms. We must have been a sight for sore eyes. Unbelievably, I had risked my family's lives to prove that I could beat Mother Nature. There is no doubt in my mind, I was certifiably insane.

We rolled into Oklahoma City just about noon. I had no idea where Bethany Hospital was located so I called out over the emergency channel on the CB for directions. Thank God, some kind soul answered my plea and directed us, remaining on the radio until we were safely at the hospital.

We hobbled up the steps to the elevators. An attendant directed us to the ICU floor. The elevator door opened onto a humongous waiting room. It must have been 3,000 square feet, with only a few chairs. Very peculiar. Everyone in my family had already assembled. We chatted briefly. Ann, my youngest sister, said that they were just waiting for Mom to die.

"I've got to see her. Who's in there now?"

"Doug is with her now. Mother seems to want him there. You can just tell by her gestures. We're taking turns. Each of us gets fifteen minutes."

"Then it's my turn. The rest of you have already had yours."

Sure enough, Doug was standing beside her bed. If he moved to the foot of the bed, her eyes followed. Somehow or another she knew it was him.

Doug was the youngest of the seven children. He was fifteen at the time. While Dad was out sleeping with every slut in town, Doug was home with Mom. He had given her CPR when she collapsed on the floor. He had the presence of mind to call 911. He was not only Mom's youngest, he was her best friend. It was easy to see why she tracked his every movement.

I could feel her tugging at me. I had been very successful up to then. It felt as though she was begging me to promise I would take care of Doug.

I called Barry, a friend of mine from the days of Aspen. Barry was a psychiatrist and a neurosurgeon. He had just moved his practice from Georgetown, DC to Miami.

"Barry, my mother is in the hospital with a cranial aneurism. The doctors say it's terminal. Mind you, this is Oklahoma. Medical practitioners are not the greatest here." I told him about how she responded to Doug.

"Ray, I can be there in two days but her doctors are correct. An aneurism is like exploding a grenade inside the skull. There is nothing left. What you are seeing when your mother looks at your brother is an involuntary response elicited by the sound and smell of her youngest baby. I'll tell you what, I'll come up and sit with your family, if that will help. But there is nothing I can do as a physician to help your mother."

"If you are sure you can't help her, there is no need for your coming. Thanks Barry, just the same."

We buried Mom three days later.

I could never erase all the bad things from my memory that Dad had done to Mom. She was aware of some of his affairs, but not all of them. I was third oldest of the seven children. My two older brothers missed out of one hell of a good time by joining the Navy early. I had traveled with my stepfather since I was sixteen, first as a chauffeur, then as a drinking buddy. He had had an affair with his secretary, which resulted in two children — all the time while he was living with my mother. There were no secrets between the two of us; I never condoned or condemned his behavior.

In my mind, the stress she lived under day-to-day was enough to kill anyone. It was Dad's fault and I knew it. So did he. My siblings had no idea of his many extramarital affairs. They'd never seen this side of the old man or, if they did, they turned their heads.

Many people in Kansas and Oklahoma knew and loved Mother. Lots of them came to her funeral, including my ex-wife, Kari. In fact, Kari rode with Annie and me.

The family and close friends gathered at a motel in Woodward, Oklahoma the day before the funeral. That night, the boys gathered in Dr. Rex's room with his wife, Helen. We each brought our favorite liquor. Rex and Helen brought a cooler full of cold beer. The mood was somber. Everyone had a bit of the alcohol glow about them.

Doug came into the room and said, "Look at you. Everyone is drinking. Mother hated that shit. Show some respect for her."

Not one person said a word. Helen poured her drink on the floor. Each of us followed suit. I don't know how Rex and Helen managed to stay in the room that night. It must have smelled like a rancid beer hall.

The church filled up with well-wishers. There was not a dry eye in the pews. We buried Mom alongside her mother and father. Her headstone was rather large, but her name was the only one engraved on it. I thought at the time, "Dad has made up his mind; he won't be buried here."

Buckling Down

Back in Dallas, my drinking spun out of control. Annie bought, I drank. December graduation was a few weeks away. My advisor reminded me I had to pass my orals first. That shocked me. I had lost track of all time. It never dawned on me that I had enough hours to graduate. I took a week off, gathered every Wall Street Journal I had ever received, and a large portion of my textbooks. For some reason, I felt it would be conducive to learning if I hid away in my aunt's house in Fort Supply — a good five-hour drive from Dallas.

Aunt Thelma welcomed me warmly, as she always did. She was a widow, with no children, and few friends.

"Auntie, I need a place to study. Could you keep my stay a secret until my last day? I promise I'll make time for the relatives then."

"Well, sure I will. Why don't you take the bed in the spare room and set up a study place in the front room?" Auntie's den was as tranquil as John the apostle's cave at Patmos.

"Perfect. See you in three days," I said.

Of the course three days was a figure of speech. She got the message, interrupting me only to invite me to eat.

But my secret didn't last through the first day. A cousin came over and wanted to talk. I listened to his woes for a good two hours, and then said "Phil, I hate to be rude, but I have to read everything that's laid out here over the next three days."

"I understand. I'll see you again before you leave. I promise."

My secret blown, I knew I was going to be bowled over with well-wishers. I was the first of multiple generations to earn a graduate degree. They couldn't have been any more proud than if I had been an astronaut.

The surprise was on me – no-one came but my uncle. He came over every morning of the week to have coffee with Auntie. Not once did he stick his head in my makeshift study to say hello. The time spent there was one of the most productive periods I ever had as a student.

The third day rolled around and I told Auntie, "The door's open. Let 'em in." Much to my surprise - or disappointment - no one came. Phil came late in the afternoon, as he had promised. We had a long chat, and shared some jug wine. It seemed like he wanted to tell me that he was "gay." I pretended not to be shocked. I think he was counting on my acceptance.

A group of professors and directors from our community college, Brookhaven, were touring our manufacturing plant. They were there to set up off-site learning facilities. Not only did they need an off-site campus, they also needed adjunct faculty. On their way out, one of them lingered behind the others.

"I'm the academic dean. Have you thought about teaching?" he asked.

"Well, yes I have. Just didn't know how to go about finding a job."

"Come and see me tomorrow. You're hired if you want the job. Classes begin in January."

"That is perfect timing. I graduate in December."

I jumped at the opportunity to teach college. I needed the money, God knows. More importantly, I needed my fix of ego juice. You can't elevate one's status in the community any more than by teaching college. I taught nights and Saturdays.

My mind was a-whirl with images of success. I had received honors on my oral exams. I was an assistant professor of business, and a respected recruiter. What more could anyone ask for?

Plenty — there was always sex. One can never get enough sex. Again, I spun out of control. This time with a well-built, brown-eyed mother of two. She was gorgeous. I think the reason I was so infatuated with Jill was because everyone else was. She was flirtatious, but in a subtle way. When she walked into the room, all eyes followed. When she walked out, the room was abuzz with chatter, giggles and fantasies.

Well, shit, if she was today's trophy, by God I had to win it. Predators are opportunists. To throw a little fuel on the fire, throw on some "mania". It was one of those times when my manic state was running on steroids. I had a pile of cash from my commodity trades, a farm, a new car and a wonderful family. "Hey Ray, let's see you fuck this up!" said the voices from within. Tally-ho. Game on!

It took some doing. First we met at the Sonic after work, then at the country club, then in one park or another. One day I coaxed her into coming to my apartment for lunch.

Both of us knew why we were there, and it wasn't for lunch. From the moment we embraced, we were on the floor. I couldn't get her panty hose off, so I pulled them down to her knees and went to work. Her vagina was so large I couldn't tell whether I was inside her or not. To this day, I've yet to screw anyone with such a cavernous pussy.

As we were walking out the door, my neighbor walked out of his apartment. He also worked at the company, but with Jill's husband. Jill slammed the door behind me, leaving me on the landing by myself. When my neighbor was out of sight, I went back inside.

Jill was pale as a ghost.

"Hey, what was that all about?"

"Your neighbor is my husband's best friend!"

We waited a few minutes, giving the guy a chance to drive off. We returned to work in total silence. Upon arrival, she jumped out of my car and dashed to the entrance door, near my office. I waited a few minutes and did the same. I totally expected her husband to call me that day. He never did.

Perhaps that's the reason I loved risky behavior so much, just the thought of being caught gives me an extra heavy dose of adrenalin.

We continued to meet wherever we could, including in one of my classes. Oh yeah, did I mention she enrolled in a class I was teaching?

My Brother's Keeper

Roger, my older brother, and I both worked for Halliburton. For some reason, he liked taking potshots at me behind the scenes. News of my relationship with Jill was not a closely guarded secret. Neither of us was ashamed of our affair, but we were both married and neither of us wanted to rub our spouse's nose in our indiscretion. Roger couldn't keep this juicy gossip from his wife. She in turn called Annie and the blame game was on.

I denied any wrongdoing. She believed me — for the moment. Roger had the facts so badly mangled, that it was not difficult for a pro like me to debunk his entire story.

About mid-semester, while at home and busy with my studies, Lori came into my office to tell me some woman was on the phone and wished to speak with me. Without thinking, I picked up the phone.

It was Jill. Her husband had found a love letter I had written to her. He threatened to divorce her, they got into a fight, and she left the house. Now she wanted to meet me somewhere.

I felt obligated, so we met in the country club parking lot. Her speech was slurred and she was trembling. I wanted to comfort her. It was my fault that she was in this mess to begin with. We fondled one another for a while, and then she began trying to suck blood out of my neck. She wanted to make love, right there in the parking lot. Finally, I got her calmed down and encouraged her to return home.

I went home too. It was warm in my office so I took off my tee shirt. Lori came in to kiss me goodnight. Annie returned from her evening classes shortly afterwards. I heard Lori get out of bed and say something to her mom. Pissed and hurt, Annie plunged through the door to my office and began looking at my neck closely.

"Ray, where did you get the hickey?"

"I don't have a hickey."

"Stop lying to me. Lori told me some woman called and then you left for an hour or so."

"That's true. A student called and asked me to meet her. We met. She was extremely agitated about some domestic problem she and her husband were having. She threw her arms around my neck. I did my best to console her. She must have kissed my neck. I don't remember."

"You are lying. Your own brother told his wife you were having an affair with a married woman with two children. She told me everything."

With my marriage on the line, my mind overflowed with self-pity. "What now? There goes the big house. Where will the children stay this summer? When will my employer find out? What will be their verdict?" The thoughts tumbled over one another.

I was guilty, but that didn't matter to me at the time. We agreed to a breakup. "Fight or take flight!" I remember one of my professors saying. This time, for me, it was flight. I had to leave. I couldn't stand the awful fact of having to look into Annie's face every day. My guilt was too much. Annie and I kissed and embraced one another. It was a sad goodbye. And, as usual, all my fault.

Jill and I broke our relationship, but not our friendship. Her husband filed for divorce and subsequently sold their house. With her take, she bought motorcycles for the two of them. I guess she did so out of guilt. This time, it was not just my marriage that went to hell, but hers as well.

"What the fuck am I doing?" I asked myself. "I keep doing the same old thing, time after time. Why?" No answer came.

Third Life or Was It Wife?

Then, like divine intervention again, a man from Allstate Insurance called me.

"Ray, my name is Joe Johnson. I am the personnel recruiter for Allstate Insurance. We met at a conference for personnel recruiters. My daughter works at Halliburton. You might know her — Leigh?"

I knew of Leigh by way of her husband, Bill. He and I shared a cubicle during my early days at Halliburton. "Of course I know Leigh. She was married to Bill. I understand they split up."

"Yes they did. She moved into a tiny apartment and wants to move into a larger one, closer to work. Do you have a pickup truck?"

"No. I lost mine in my own divorce."

"Do you know someone you might borrow one from?"

"I sure do. One of my friends has a new one. I hired him. He owes me."

"I also need a little help. Some of her stuff I can't handle by myself. I'll pay."

"I'd be glad to help. Forget about the money. How long do you think it'll take?"

"Maybe an hour or so."

"Joe, just call me when you are ready. Weekends are best for me."

"How about this Saturday? Let's say around 9:00 a.m., is that okay?"

"Give me the address. We'll meet you there. What's her apartment number?"

Leigh didn't have a lot to move. Some end tables, food, clothes and a bed. Her apartment was a bit cluttered, but I thought nothing of it.

"Where are we to take this, Joe?"

"Just follow me."

He pulled into my apartment complex. He stopped in front of the very building I lived in.

"Shit, we are going to be neighbors."

It didn't take long to unload. Mike, a co-worker, and I bid them farewell and went to my apartment for a beer. About the third beer, I heard a knock. I answered, thinking it might be a friend from school. Standing there in full winter regalia was Leigh.

"May I come in?" she asked.

"Of course. Make yourself at home."

"May I have a beer?"

"Mike. Get this lady a beer."

We discussed our divorces/breakups while finishing another six-pack of Coors. By the time she left, I felt as though I had known her all my life. And she me.

Mike and I were three sheets to the wind. Mike said, "Ray, you always seem to get all the beautiful girls. What is it about you?"

Mike was right, it did appear that generally the women I dated or married were beautiful, at least to me. A pretty girl can't say "no" any faster than a plain girl, so if you're going to play, you might as well play with the best teammates. One has to be in the game to win, and I was always "in the game".

Winter of 1978 was when the great ice storm hit Dallas. My brother Roger, Leigh, and I had all recently moved out of our comfortable homes into small apartments. The first cold night, there was a tap on the door.

"Hey, what a pleasant surprise. What are you doing, Leigh?

"It's cold in my apartment. I can't sleep. Is yours any warmer?" she asked.

"Drink enough scotch and they all seem warm. Want some?"

"I'm not much of a scotch drinker. I'll try it. Pour me a little," she said.

My definition of "small" was an 8 oz glass half-filled with booze. It took her several sips, but she caught on quickly. It was not long before she was spurting out her entire life's story.

The more she drank, the more she chattered — and the harder my dick got. I had just met her a few days ago. "Should I ask her to bed? What have I got to lose? If I ask her and she says no, she'll leave me alone. If she says yes, I'll have another filly in my stable." I had it all figured out.

"You want to sleep here tonight?"

"Where?" she asked.

"In my bed!"

"Okay. I need to get my toothbrush and nightie," she said.

"You won't need your nightgown."

We giggled nervously. While she was gathering her toiletries, I brushed my teeth, combed my hair and slipped into some pajama bottoms. She was back in less than ten minutes.

She looked at me in my PJs and said, "You're kind of in a hurry, aren't you?"

"Yeah. It's too cold. Let's crawl under the comforter and warm up."

I grabbed her hand and led her to my bed like she was a little puppy. We may not have had one of my three-hour lays, but we sure made a good two hours of it. Both of us were exhausted, and fell asleep in one another's arms. I didn't try to poke her again until sun up. I simply nudged her. Leigh rolled over and smiled at me. I slipped my legs between hers. Her broad smile broadcast her approval. And so went the entire first half of that day.

"I can't get enough of you. I could stay inside you all day long."

"Well then, do it. You don't hear me complaining," she said.

"I hope you take the pill. I'd hate like hell to get you pregnant."

"I don't have to take a pill. My doctor told me I could never have children. That is partly to blame for my divorce with Bill. He wanted children and I couldn't give him any."

We made love most of the morning, although we didn't bang all the time. She seemed satisfied. Actually, it was very cozy. Nothing seems to warm a man's innards more than dipping his tool inside a warm vagina.

Day of Glory

I passed my oral exams with honors. I did so well that my advisor excused me from the last class days, as well as the finals. He told all the classes that he had just come from one of the most interesting orals he had ever sat though. Dr. Presley didn't mention me by name, but the other students told me they knew I was the only one scheduled for orals that week. The grand review established my status in the academic and industry circles over the next five years. I was drunk on ego. It's damn hard to fly when one is so full of himself he can't take off.

Well, here it was, graduation time, and I had no one to go with. I invited several girls from work, and I never heard so many "no's" in my life. One right after the other. Here I was a "big hero" and no girl wanted to go with me. One hell of a change.

It finally dawned on me that Leigh might want to go. I asked, she agreed. Mike, my good friend, volunteered his services. Between the two of us, we concocted a great scheme. I would purchase a case of champagne. Mike would drive the black Cadillac and Leigh and I could sit in the back and sip champagne.

It worked like a champ. We sipped and guzzled Cold Duck from Dallas to Commerce, about fifty miles to the east. By the time we reached the school, I was totally wasted.

Leigh took over. "Let's go find your cap and gown."

"Hey, don't forget to ask them where I am supposed to place my tassel." Bachelors have a certain position. Masters have another, and doctorates yet another. Too confusing for an ole country boy.

She came back to our dressing room within minutes with cap, gown and tassel in hand.

"Make sure you remember to place your tassel to the left of the center. After you are handed your diploma, move it the right side. That signals you're moving from a bachelor's to a master's."

"Remind me before I cross the stage," I laughed.

Leigh's motherly instinct warmed me to the core. We had one hell of a party that night. She earned a special place in my heart. She sacrificed a day's pay, gave up a night's sleep (and a lot of pussy), and escorted me through graduation exercises. All that and beautiful as well.

Rookie Error

Winter 1979 was the virgin semester for the newest building on campus. Everything was new — even the smell. The first night on my new teaching job, I brought my own dry erase markers from work, thinking the school wouldn't have enough.

After a brief introduction, I settled in. My nerves had calmed somewhat and my hands were not shaking as badly as before the class. I was now the "sage on the stage". I went directly into my expectations, class outline, assignments and the syllabus. Then I launched into the lesson.

I started at the left of the rather long board. When I finished writing, I was at the far right. Just to make sure the students got my meaning, I used colored markers to emphasize certain sections. I gave the students a brief period to finish taking notes from the board and began erasing from the left. But it didn't work.

"Oh shit!"

The eraser wasn't erasing. I wiped again. Nothing. I wetted the eraser a little and tried again. Still nothing. The board was a genuine chalk board, and not the marker type. The ink from the markers was there to stay. I thought my heart was going to explode.

For the remainder of the year, I had to see my blunder three times a week. Amazingly, not one person said a word about the incident — they didn't have to. The right thing to do would have been to replace the board, at my own expense. However, this was no ordinary chalkboard. First it was brown, not the usual green. Next, it covered the entire length of the front wall of the classroom. Too expensive for my meager budget.

I always wondered if the school ever replaced that board.

Unwelcome Surprise

I managed to bask in the glory for the next several months. The story my professor had relayed to my fellow students about me was retold endlessly. It was wearing a little thin — even for an egomaniac such as me.

Leigh relished being a part of my success. Her father began referring to me as "that Mensa friend of Leigh's."

"How cool is that shit? Let the insanity begin!" I thought.

From the very beginning, there was a special connection between the two of us. First, our chance meeting seemed divinely inspired. Plus, she was a knockout — 5' 6", long blonde hair, and beautiful green eyes. Although she was extremely loyal, her integrity had some chinks in it.

For instance, she had already told me, "I can't get pregnant. Hope you aren't expecting children." Three months later she was pregnant. I wasn't surprised. I never believed her to begin with. First "chink" in her armor.

"Ray. I missed my period for the first time in my life. Will you pick up one of those home test kits on your way here?"

"I'm screwed!" I mused. Less than an hour after arriving home, she rendered the verdict. The test was positive. She was pregnant.

"Well, you've got to see a real doctor. If you are pregnant, you will need a good OB/Gynecologist."

"I'll call around and see who my friends recommend."

"Okay."

As usual, I began wandering about, straying a bit from our cozy little relationship. Within two months of broadcasting her pregnancy, I was back in Annie's "bed." I say "bed" because it was actually a patio swing.

Even I could see the irony in my behavior. The same old mental committee began taunting me. "Boy, are you fucked up? What's with you? A bit starved for approval, are you? To make things worse, you're a drunk!"

The voices were right. Why wasn't I satisfied with just one woman — at least with just one at a time?

During Leigh's pregnancy, I had three sexual interludes. It was inexplicable. I had morphed into my father – an exact clone. I was trapped — two prior divorces, two children with another on the way, and other women in the wings.

MBA Whiz Kid

I was legendary within my inner circle of friends. I'd made big money in the commodity market, graduated at the top of my class, and was an unabashed playboy. It was some high. I couldn't understand why I was high, but I was. One good fortune after another, they just fell my way. I certainly had done nothing to merit any of them — quite the contrary. It was baffling, even to me.

One of my ex-employees called me. "Ray, this is Charles. Remember me?"

"Of course. What's up?"

"I work for the Southland Corp. They own the 7-11's. They have a Tidel manufacturing plant two blocks east of you. We are looking for a plant manager and your name came to mind. Got any interest?"

"I might. Who is the contact person?"

A five thousand dollar salary increase and a production manager's position in a billion dollar company. What a head rush. The ink on my sheepskin hadn't even dried and here I was, a department manager.

The new job came with lots of perks: a fleet of business jets, an executive bar atop the Southland building off Stemons Freeway; quarterly bonuses, and tons of recognition.

It wasn't long before I orchestrated a fabulous success. Tidel made steel security safes for the 7-11 convenience stores. The company was bleeding cash profusely, it didn't take an MBA to see that. Production was in shambles, as was quality. One hundred employees produced 100 sales units each month — one unit for each employee.

I turned this small company on a dime. I flipped the situation so rapidly it made heads spin. We went from a hundred units per month to 1,200 units per month, with no increase in employees. Quality increased by over 100%. The staff's performance bonuses went from zero to receiving maximum bonuses within 120 days of my arrival. Life was good. Ego was fat.

Then corporate stepped in. They began questioning our high production figures — while production was high, cash flow was low. What I had not been informed of was that all the equipment I had put on trucks was not sold — it had gone to leased warehouses in Oklahoma. The parent company, Southland, had a policy to consider everything shipped within the month as having been sold. They were a "perishable" company — sandwiches, bread, milk, eggs. Products were either sold or dumped at some point within the month (generally within the week).

It goes without saying they changed that archaic policy. Production came to a halt until the inventory could be reduced — actually sold, this time. By then we had about a six months' supply. I had taken production from a hundred safes a month to over 1,200. Now we had to somehow reverse this. Southland offered the executive team jobs in other Southland plants, but their pay was too low for me. I needed an increase, not a reduction.

Off to the races. I attended all the job fairs I could fit into my schedule. One day after interviewing with companies I wanted to work for, I walked by a rather busy conference. There was a sign at the door: "McDonnell Douglas." I recognized the name immediately, so I decided to make a cold call.

Ted, a stocky man with a great tan, approached me. After a few moments - not time enough to read of all my long list of successes - he said, "You're what I'm looking for! Come see me in Long Beach. I want you to meet the rest of the staff. Mac will send you the airline tickets and an itinerary."

"I'll be there," I said. "When?"

"Give me a week to get home. I'll have personnel make reservations. You need at least one day for the interview and another to look for housing. And, of course you'll have to pass through personnel as well."

As promised, I flew to Long Beach for my interview with Ted's staff. After a tour, my mind was off to the races. This had to be a high-salaried job. Ted took me to lunch where we had a scotch and chatted.

"Ray, don't worry about the entry level of pay. Personnel have this thing about paying low for all new hires. We plan to start you as a senior manufacturing engineer. I'll get you promoted within ninety days. Just play along with them."

I still thought this was going to be a high-paying job — after all, McDonnell Douglas was recognized worldwide as a leader in the aviation industry.

After lunch, Ted showed me his office and the office where I would be working. We bid each other farewell. On my way out he said, "Personnel will be in touch with you within a week. They will tell you your starting salary and start day. Now go find a house for your family."

"My God. I can't believe my fortune. I've got to be the luckiest person on the face of this planet," I thought. I couldn't wait to tell Leigh about my day. We were both concerned about finding another job before the baby came. We had to have insurance.

Housing was high, but I found a split-level condo of sorts one block off Newport Beach — a very nice area and near the plant. On the way home, I had a lot to think about. I could see no negatives. Everything looked great. One week passed and still no letter from personnel. I called Ted and told him. He advised me to be patient. It was in the works.

Two weeks passed and I was beginning to think that Ted had made a commitment he didn't have the authority to carry out. I began searching for other jobs in Dallas. As luck would have it, Pitney Bowes was taking applications for an operations manager. I submitted my résumé and waited with bated breath. I didn't have much time left. We were running out of savings.

Then one day, my phone rang. It was Pitney Bowes, not McDonnell Douglas.

"We would like to interview you for the operations position. Can you come see us tomorrow around ten-ish?"

"I'll be there," I answered.

Ten o'clock on the dot, I was there. The receptionist directed me to the hiring manager. After a thirty-minute meeting, the manager asked me when I could start. I was on my pink cloud again.

Then came the much-anticipated call from McDonnell Douglas' personnel recruiter. The offer was a meager $36,000. More than I had ever made, but not enough for an MBA. I didn't even call Ted. I knew I couldn't afford the job in Long Beach. Housing would have cost me 25% of my salary.

First of the week rolled around before I knew it. I didn't have to move to California. Pay was about the same as the McDonnell Douglas's offer, but the commute to Pitney from my apartment was only fifteen minutes. I loved the job. It didn't take long to catch on to my duties and acquaint myself with my staff. I even introduced a couple of original ideas, which they implemented without confrontation.

Corporate Fun and Games

In the Fall, Leigh had announced she was pregnant with our first child, but in order to get health insurance, we had to be married. With the pay increase and an executive job, I felt secure enough to marry her. We wed February 1980 and Leigh became my third wife.

She gave birth to the cutest little girl I ever laid eyes on. She looked exactly like her mother — blond hair and a warm smile (I have black hair). We were not expecting a girl — actually, I am not sure what we were expecting. We walked the halls of the OB ward searching the hanging pictures for a good name.

"Leigh. Come take a look at this one," I said.

"Kelsey? What type of name is that?"

"Hell, I don't know. But I like the sound of it," I answered.

Kelsey it was. We were so excited to take Kelsey home. Added to my great job was a beautiful little bundle of joy. This put an end to my philandering — for a while, anyhow. We did everything within our power to spoil that baby. What we didn't buy her, her grandparents did. Within two years, a rash of parents began naming their baby girls "Kelsey" — a trend that lasted for over a decade. I construed this as another blessing from God.

Everything was wine and roses. I could do no wrong. My manufacturing plant at Pitney moved from its old building into a newer one. My responsibilities expanded. My boss won a coveted job at one of the larger plants in Connecticut. I felt sure I would fill his position. After all, by anyone's standards, I had revolutionized my previous operation. It didn't happen. Instead of promoting me, they demoted a long term VP to the position. The VP, Bob, was deeply hurt with the demotion he had been dealt.

It was the 1980s and the national economy was on a downturn. Pitney implemented an austerity program. Rental cars, fancy hotels, monthly lunches, all went to the wayside. A senior executive was assigned to our plant as president — further irritating Bob. Then came the feared reduction in forces. Some long-term employees were swept up in the layoffs. One such employee was friends with Bob, who became belligerent, openly criticizing the Pitney Bowes Corporation as a whole.

Word leaked back to me that Bob told the old-timer that the new president had better watch his ass. As opposed to using a taxi or a rental car, the new president walked to work from his hotel when in town. After all, using either would have been sacrilege after telling everyone else that they were not to be used. The story I got was that Bob also said he would shoot the son-of-a-bitch if he (the president) messed with him.

After some gut wrenching deliberation, I took the information I had to our personnel manager. I made it quite clear that it was hearsay, second-hand information. I went on to say that it was just Bob's way of voicing his displeasure with the new arrangements. Nevertheless, I would have been remiss if I didn't report what I had heard.

Word quickly traveled to Connecticut. Later that week, they fired Bob. Again, I thought I was in line to be promoted to at least the position vacated by Bob. It didn't happen.

Some months later, Bob committed suicide in a public park. He had all his rifles with him — about a dozen in total, or so the newspaper reported.

The Crash

In 1982, just about when Kelsey turned two, I began yet another employment search. It was kind of like chasing a woman and I started liking the pursuit. First came an offer from the Cherokee Tribe located in eastern Oklahoma, then one from an oil and gas drill bit manufacturer located in Houston. I choose the job in Houston — principally because it paid $65,000. The company, NL Hycalog, was a small division of a large conglomerate, NL Industries.

I was well on the way to realizing my goal of becoming an executive with a Fortune 500 company. I hit it off with everyone in the division and, more importantly, within the mother company. Everything was peachy again. Another extreme high on the horizon.

Then the 1983 depression in the Gulf oil patch hit. Oil dropped precipitously from $44 per barrel to $25 per barrel. Corporate-wide, employment exceeded 26,000. The chairman of the board sent in a retired VP from by-gone days. This old fart had a reputation which preceded him. If anyone dragged his/her feet or so much as questioned his methodology, he'd say, "Hand me the phone. I want to hear you tell the chairman what you just told me!" End of confrontation.

I was a survivor. While the corporation pared 20,000 employees from their payroll and boarded up numerous plants, I remained comfortably at home. I had worked my way up to the advisory committee that decided what divisions were to be shut down and which employees were to be discharged.

After work, drinking was the order of the day. Everyone wanted to know who was on the cutting board. I had pledged not to reveal a word spoken in the advisory meetings. These meetings were held each morning at 5:30. Shit, most of us were still reeling from the alcohol consumed the night before. The drinking often continued until the bars closed at 2:00 a.m. That gave us three hours to sober up. Not a chance.

Things settled down a bit after we had disassembled nine out of ten divisions. Our division hired a new President from Cummins Engine Co. He brought in very few ideas. As a matter of fact, he spent his lunch hour with the personnel manager researching and trading stocks.

We managed to dismantle nearly all of the oil- and gas-related manufacturing companies. My small plant incorporated three additional major manufacturing plants. Before the economic downturn, each of these plants used to employ hundreds of people.

We were looking for the exit doors, and I was on the street again.

Student Bodies

Winter term 1983, I found a part-time job as a professor at a nearby college. That was great. The "small" community college had an enrollment of 11,000. One of our main objectives was to keep the seats filled. Then there was the additional goal of keeping the students in class until after the twelfth day of class. If a student dropped prior to the twelve-day hurdle, the state wouldn't fund the school for the pupil. Not a problem for me. After the first semester, my classes filled quickly.

It was no time before I had a whole gaggle of female students in hot pursuit. One in particular caught my attention. She was a single mother. Candy - as she was called, with good reason - was a hot momma indeed. About midway through the semester, we hooked up. She began accompanying me on weekend field trips to the oil fields.

She was the first and last nymphomaniac in my life. Yeah. I fucked her. What would you have done? I had never had sex with a real-life nympho prior to Candy. Our relationship continued to grow, but my desire began to wane. I couldn't keep up with her. It got to the point where she would call my secretary, asking to speak with me. My secretary was in another office, but answered all incoming calls. One day Candy called and Lisa, my secretary, transferred the call but didn't hang up the phone.

"Want to come to my place and fuck for lunch?" Candy blurted out.

"Hey. I told you never to call me at work. I have a demanding schedule. We can talk about it after class tonight."

She was obviously disappointed with my remark. Nevertheless, we continued our relationship throughout the semester. In addition to being a mistress by night, she helped me grade tests and record grades. She actually was a great helper. Then she would fuck me to death in lieu of payment.

She became so stimulated during sex that her womb went into convulsions. I could feel — and hear —

the slurping of her vagina. Great sound, but definitely out of the ordinary. She exacted as many orgasms as she could from me. It left me weak-kneed. And she still wanted more.

Candy also had a thing for oral sex. "I'll give you a blow job if you'll eat me."

She told me her entire sexual life, beginning when her mother caught her and her boyfriend having sex on the sofa one night. She was sixteen.

"What did she say?" I pried.

"Not one word. Not even the next day. One day I was riding in the car with a cowboy. I don't know what came over us, but he slammed on the brakes and we jumped out of the car and had sex right there in the grass."

And so it went.

Things got worse. One Saturday morning while working in my office, Lisa, my secretary, came in. She was not wearing a bra and her silk blouse clung to her small breasts. This was totally uncharacteristic for Lisa. She was always so proper.

"Lisa, what brings you in on a Saturday?" I asked.

"I was just driving by and saw your car. Is there anything I can do to help you?"

She smiled and then turned a bit red. She was blushing — something I had never seen her do in the three years we had worked together.

I knew she was lying. She lived about fifteen miles from the office and had no reason to be in the area other than to seduce me.

"Oh shit. She is not here to help. She wants to fool around. She has been eavesdropping on my calls," I said to myself. "As much as I need a little sex, I have to remain composed."

"Lisa, that is very kind of you. However, I am just about through with this and need to go home and eat. Thanks just the same. I really appreciate your offer."

We never had that conversation again.

Then there was a young beauty who sat in the front row of my class, next to the wall. She said, "My car is overheating. I don't think I can make it home. Can you help me?"

"Drop by my house after class. I'll look at it. Perhaps it just needs water," I said.

I didn't give it another thought. I had another class to teach that evening and assumed she had one more to attend. Big mistake. When I got home, around ten that evening, her car was in my driveway. She and my wife were having a chat about me. Leigh had her nightgown on. Leigh just glared at me. I had been had.

"What in hell can I do?" I asked myself.

I excused myself and went to her car. I poured some water in the radiator and told her she needed to have the thing cleaned and there was nothing more I could do. That ended that little tryst. Even when I was trying to be good, women chased after me. And then another. And another.

An extremely sexy student sat directly in front of my desk (the seduction zone). Teresa enjoyed spreading her legs and slouching down in her chair so I could see all the way to her ass. Then she would look into my eyes to see if she was getting through to me. She was a teaser. I did my best to resist my temptation — and hers as well.

About two months after the semester ended, Teresa showed up at my Pitney Bowes office. "Teresa, what are you doing here, you little fox?"

"One of your managers hired me. I am a full time employee here now," she replied.

My heart was pounding so hard I thought I was going to hyperventilate. "How am I going to cope with this? She can get my ass fired," I said to myself.

Each morning, instead of taking her coffee break with the others, Teresa came to my office. I had no idea how to persuade her to stop. I didn't much want to either. After looking up her skirt the entire semester, I was a bit curious about how her little fur box looked — not to mention how it felt. The daily meetings turned to daily doses of flirtations, one trying to gain an advantage over the other — then to foreplay.

One day I asked, "Why don't you go with me this weekend? I've got to deliver some products in Oklahoma. I've got a farm near where the oil rig is located. We can stay there."

"Ray, I just might surprise you. What if I said yes?'

"Go ahead. Surprise me. By the way, what color panties do you have on today? I really miss looking up your skirt."

"They're red. Do you like red?"

"Oh yeah? Red is my favorite! Show me."

Teresa looked over her shoulder to see if anyone was watching. She stepped into my office and pulled her dress up just enough to reveal her crotch. I thought I was going to rip off her panties and throw her across my desk. If we had been alone, I would have.

And where was my wife during all this? At home, taking care of our children, of course.

Something twisted was going on inside my mind, something I couldn't control.

Drilling for Dollars

Dick, our new divisional president at N.L. Hycalog, told me one day in the spring of '84 to inventory every piece of excess stock we had on hand.

"Analyze the list and find those items that we no longer use. Then go after those that move, but slowly. Don't overlook used items. I want you to find a place for these items. I don't care if you make boat trailers. Just find something that will generate cash flow, above and beyond what we already have."

This was right up my alley. As a small child growing up on a dirt farm in western Oklahoma, I used to find old rusty objects, such as corn huskers, jacks, horse bridles, and plow shears then clean the rust and dirt from them with a wire brush and paint them. On Saturdays, when my grandparents went to town to sell their excess milk and pick up some staples, I would go to the local beer joints and sell these items. This little venture was quite successful. I used the proceeds to buy clothes and other products I thought I could resell.

The first thing that came to mind was to take worn out drilling bits and weld a pipe inside the throat of the bit. I began selling these as mailbox stands. In the overall scheme of things, that was but a drop in the bucket.

Then I stumbled across the idea of re-manufacturing worn out drilling bits. My thought was to remove the parts that were actually worn out, and reuse the leftovers to manufacture a new product.

It was an instant hit. In the beginning, I had to do my own machining, which I knew absolutely nothing about. The company loaned me a few seasoned machinists. We mapped out what we wanted to accomplish. We were a real rag-tag "Sanford and Son" operation. Within six months, I employed six engineers (all retired or laid off from other companies), a metallurgist, a draftsman, several machinists and an unlimited budget.

We sold excess material to generate our cash requirements. MIT took notice of our project. Cummins Engine began to take interest. They owned a $200M division in Memphis that specialized in re-manufacturing diesel engines. Cummins ReCon was the leader in re-manufacturing used equipment. It was a perfect fit. They offered to fund my project with $250,000. Along with their cash came an extremely intelligent engineer. He was a graduate of General Motors Institute. I don't believe he had any limitations. Not only was he gifted, but he also liked to drink. With his help and Cummins money, we leaped ahead. Within months after their involvement, we had discovered a method to accomplish our goals.

We now had the interest of NL Industries, the parent company, including the president. With help from Cummins, we finalized our methodology, tested the product both in the field and in NL's testing laboratory, and earned two patents in the process. Then our division president resigned to go to work for WW Grainger, a nationwide industrial supply house. He was my best ally — my mentor. I knew I'd miss him.

Then the dreaded day came. Cummins agreed to take over my project and pay NL an additional $250,000.

"Ray," the new president said, "Cummins purchased your project."

"That is great! I said all along that I would build a company out of it. What is my next project?"

"There is no 'next' project. You will be going with the new company."

"Why wasn't I asked about this beforehand? I don't want to go!" I said.

"Then you are fired. Your next paycheck will come to the Cummins's address."

He gave me the address and told me I had thirty days to move my personnel and equipment into the new facility. It was located on the ship channel in south Houston, about a 45-minute drive for me.

I couldn't afford to lose my sole source of income, so I accepted the job with Cummins. Thank God for that. Divine intervention, I guess. We named the new company after our new owner, Cummins ReCon. It took less than six months to recruit a handful of independent distributors. They were not paid a salary, nor were their expenses paid.

Instead, I offered them a 15% commission. Not too shoddy considering the product sold for $2,500-plus.

It didn't take long to sell out our total capacity. We needed more equipment and additional personnel. I was handed what amounted to a blank check and told to find some equipment. Cummins also included my division on the distribution list for excess machine tools. The first shopping spree — an auction in Ontario, CA.

The Federal Bankruptcy Court forced one of our competitors into receivership. This company used the same equipment I needed. I purchased a 40-foot trailer load of well-maintained machine tools, hand tools, forgings, intellectual properties, and machine fixtures that were worth their weight in gold. With the help of a local wino from San Jose, we loaded the equipment in about an hour. I contracted a local transportation broker to ship the equipment to Houston using "least expensive" method. Rail just happened to be the cheapest. We loaded the truck in such a hurry that it looked like a pack rat's nest. By the time it arrived in Houston, pieces of equipment were protruding through the sides of the truck. It never dawned on me just how rough the ride on a rail could be. Hobos must be damn desperate to hitch a cross-country ride on one of those bitches.

Over the next half a decade, I rode a high much as a surfer rides a gigantic wave. It was the most exhilarating thing I ever imagined. The taste of success was all around. This was my sanctuary. This was the ride of my life.

Hitting Bottom

I was not much of a husband or father during those years, choosing instead to work at my office or in the oil field. Relations began to strain — again. Drinking was the only thing that remained constant.

But my drinking finally caught up with me. In November of 1991, Cummins fired me and offered rehab if I consented.

"First of all, I am not a drunk," or so I thought. "Every drink I took was in the name of business development." That was my explanation to my wife, who had worn quite tired of my excuses, my denial. I passed on the rehab offer.

I spent the next year as a consultant, working for one client then another. I became well known. My fees were reasonable and my recommendations spot-on. Some days I worked around the clock, stopping only long enough to catch a wink of sleep. Leigh would bring me a bottle of Jack Daniels some evenings to help me through the night. By sun-up, I found myself waiting in line at Kinko's to have my report or valuation printed and bound. Then off to the client's office.

I knew going into the consulting business that I had to be paid for every job. I began by asking for cash up front. It worked. Returning clients knew I was a man of my word.

In the interim, I badgered Leigh into taking some college courses. She hated me for it — and never failed to let me know. Much to my surprise and her diligence, she completed her bachelors in English and vowed to get her masters, but she never pursued it.

The recession in the oil and gas industry spilled over into the general economy. Consulting jobs dried up. I became one of the casualties. With no job and no prospects on the horizon, I filed for unemployment.

Leigh worked to feed the children. After the years as an executive, I now had to apply for food stamps. It was the deepest point of despair in my life. I couldn't feed my family without social assistance. The children came home one day after school and informed us that the school social worker gave them each vouchers for school lunches. This was the first time that they realized we were on welfare. I don't know why, but Leigh stuck with me. She earned my respect — a great stride from where our relationship was when we first met.

Somewhere along the way, I noticed a change in Leigh's behavior. "She is having an affair with someone at her office," I surmised. A male friend from her company began calling our house. They talked at length — about what, I'll never know.

Lean and Mean

Finally, in April of '92, I landed a VP position with a well-known Fortune 500 company in Houston. The money was not great, but what it lacked in salary, they made up for in prestige and perks. I wasted no time in remolding the company into what I envisioned. My staff railed against me. At every corner, they would call for an intervention with our CEO, my superior.

I was implementing "lean manufacturing," something I had learned well while at Cummins — I just didn't call it that. The label itself was a big red flag to those who knew about it. Richard, my manufacturing engineer manager, told me one day, "Ray, I know you are taking tremendous heat for what you are trying to do. A Frenchman wrote a book titled Chaos. In managing chaos, one stirs up all the balls. When you get them in the air, you reposition the balls into a morphed new organization. I know it works, if you don't drop one of the balls. You can count on me for support."

Richard was just the ally I needed. I turned their manufacturing around. I even got to go to Jamaica on a company gig to promote new product and services. The CEO arranged for me to present my successes to our distributors. Leigh was also invited. What a high. I was not drinking, humbled by my fall into poverty. Leigh had trimmed down enough to fit in a bikini again. She looked great and was a hit with my associates and our clients. Life was good.

My presentation went off without a hitch. Afterwards, The CEO's wife approached the two of us and told us how impressed her husband and the attendees were with what I had accomplished in such a short time.

Back in Houston, a potential customer requested a tour of our plant prior to doing business with us. I was the guide; after all, it was "my" plant. The customer was impressed. He told me, "I am going to sign on with your company. Tell your marketing people operations made the sale."

"I appreciate that. Could you tell the CEO instead?"

"Damn right I will."

So went another round of accolades. I was the in-house expert. The chairman of the board called to compliment me. He began sending influential people and college students to our plant. By now, I was well-entrenched.

Shortly thereafter, my staff convened a fourth intervention. They had heard enough about "lean manufacturing" to know that the end-goal was to reduce workers as well as inventory. Each day brought a new rumor about layoffs. The employees and my staff in particular, were swarming like a nest of hornets in a hail storm. Enough was enough. I began looking for other employment. As well connected as I was, I had learned not to wait until the hammer fell. Make a preemptive strike. Leave them before they leave you. It reminded me of my marriages.

Summer 1992 brought good news as one of my old friends with the Cherokee Nation called with an offer. I received a $12,000 salary increase, but also the titles I had longed for — COO and CFO. "Shit yeah, I am going." Now came the hard part, telling my CEO that I was leaving. He had defended me so many times — how could I desert him? It wasn't easy, but it was what I needed to do.

Within two weeks, I was in Oklahoma working for the Cherokees. Leigh remained in Houston, not wanting to move the children until school let out for summer vacation.

My father warned me. "You're taking one hell of a risk. Most marriages don't last through one of these transitions." I didn't heed his advice.

Grand Canyon Adventure

Prior to moving to Oklahoma, Leigh and I planned a trip to the Grand Canyon with several friends from Houston. We were all to meet up with some other friends from Phoenix and Albuquerque at the canyon.

Leigh and a fellow manager-friend of mine from the N.L. Hycalog era left Houston together. I met them in Phoenix. Leigh and I leased a convertible and made the drive to the park the next day. My friend rode with his daughter.

The drive was beautiful. We stopped along the road to shop for curios and hiking gear — just a leisurely drive. We arrived at the lodge at the rim of the canyon around noon. The others met us for dinner. We agreed to convene at a popular cafeteria near one of the trails at 6:00 the next morning for breakfast, prior to embarking on our hike.

A group of elders sat next to us at breakfast. One of the men in their group had a giant freshly-skinned place on the left side of his face. I just had to ask him how he got it.

"I fell down on the trail yesterday and slid down an embankment," he said.

That was the last thing I wanted to hear. I was already apprehensive about the descent into the canyon — it was our first trip down. We had made reservations at the Phantom Ranch, which sits along the banks of the Colorado River.

Following breakfast, we checked our gear and headed to South Kaibab Trail. There were twelve of us, ranging in age from 72 to 18. We caught the shuttle from the restaurant to the trail entrance, or at least to where we thought the entrance was supposed to be.

We got off the bus with all our belongings and walked the railing. My friends had hiked these trails many times over the past decade. I assumed they knew just where to go.

They had no idea. Like little ducklings, we fell in line behind the female lawyer from Kingwood, Texas. Like any good lawyer, she acted as if she knew exactly where she was going. She began looking to her left and then her right. She hopped over the rail and started walking toward a brushy knoll. We followed. She stopped and looked around again. I looked at the terrain and saw no trail — just a steep slope leading to nowhere.

"Oh shit," I thought. "We're going to have to rappel down this cliff to get to the trail."

Neither Leigh nor I had ever rappelled. Just when I thought my blood pressure was about to blow the top of my head off, we noticed another group descending just to the east of us. Thank God! Our lawyer lost her job as group leader.

I thought, "Fantastic, this is a great hiking trail. Plenty of room and a small handrail. No problem." Ten minutes later the palms of our hands were dripping with perspiration. I never saw such a narrow trail in all my hiking days. The guardrail was just for show. After about 50 feet, it disappeared, leaving only a rock cliff on one side and one hell of a drop-off on the other.

We made it to the plains area around noon. This was more like it. The plateau had bio facilities, and plenty of them. They smelled like shit, but then again, what is a shithouse supposed to smell like? The women felt they had to make their obligatory piss before continuing our descent ever deeper into the abyss.

As the day dragged on and the sun slipped further behind the canyon rim, members of the group dispersed, according to their skill levels. Leigh and I were on our own. We didn't know where we were or even if we were still on the right trail, but we forged ahead. At places, the path was so narrow, we walked single-file, hugging the cliff every step of the way. We kept reassuring each other that all was okay. We would make it in due time.

Late in the afternoon, after a hair-raising day of cliff hugging, we spotted the pedestrian bridge over the Colorado. A suspension bridge, it appeared to be just in front of us. Phantom Ranch was just beyond the north side of the bridge, so we were near camp — or so we thought. It took another hour or so to reach the bridge. We thought we had seen some horrific trails, but this bridge swung sickeningly back and forth above the river. At least it had handrails.

About 5:00 p.m. we walked into the campground. The entourage shared one dorm style cabin - two bedrooms filled with twin bunk beds and one commode. The women slept in one room, the men in the other. A common bathhouse was located about fifty yards north of our cabin, for those with enough energy to walk to it.

Leigh and I were walking as though we had been riding mules all day. Every muscle in my body ached. I never knew it could be so painful walking down a mountain. We met a French couple who just arrived in the camp. They pitched a tent and cooked their own meal. We told them how sore we were, expecting a little sympathy.

"We have walked all over Europe and hiked the Alps. Nothing compares to this one. I guess it comes from walking down hill for seven hours. We generally walk uphill, then downhill, then up and down. Never have we spent an entire day walking down hill."

Although it was not much consolation, we felt a bit better about our own misery.

Pushing Through Pain

The restaurant at Phantom Ranch is a large, one room, family style log cabin, filled with picnic tables and long benches. The food could have been dried worms but it tasted like a choice sirloin kabob. I can't remember a more satisfying meal. By the time we finished eating, we were exhausted. We headed for our cabin and turned in. I never heard such raucous snoring in my entire life! The "old" men were the loudest; to make it worse, we shared only the one room. The women's side was about as loud.

Realizing the trip back to the rim of the canyon was going to be living hell, Leigh and I decided to get up at first daylight and head on out. We picked up a bag of snacks at the "ranch house" and headed up Bright Angel Trail. The scenery along the way was spectacular. Off in the distance, mountain goats bounced from one boulder to another, stopping to graze on the sparse vegetation. The trail was considerably wider than that on Kaibab. Even the slope was gentler. It kind of made me wonder why we didn't take Bright Angel on our hike down. Then again, we would have missed one hell of an adventure.

The nearest bio area was located at Indian Camp, about three miles up from Phantom Ranch. We stopped there long enough to eat an apple, a handful of trail-mix and drain our bladders. Off to the side, Leigh spotted a helicopter.

"Is that for hauling wounded people out of the canyon?" she asked.

"I don't know. Ask someone."

She did. A hiker said, "The helicopter is used more often than not to haul tired people out; not to evacuate injured hikers. The ride will set you back $450.00." We didn't think any more about it.

About an hour up the trail from Indian Camp, we were both huffing and puffing strenuously. The incline was somewhere between twelve and fifteen degrees. For two smokers, that was a bit much. It got to the point where all our friends, who had left the camp an hour later than we did, were passing us by.

Lonnie (Doc), one of my oldest and dearest friends from our days at Hycalog, was in our group. The guy had a medical practice near the Grand Canyon and hiked the trails regularly. He buzzed by us at a trot. We would move a hundred yards or so, and there he would be perched above on a boulder like one of those goats, looking down on us, making sure we were still healthy enough to make it out. Directly behind Doc was an elderly couple from Texas. They were in their early seventies. When we caught up with them, they were sitting on the side of the trail with a red and white checkered tablecloth spread out on the ground. Unbelievable! They were eating brie cheese and having some vintage wine. Now that was the epitome of insult to the two of us. Later they told us they had recently bicycled across Belize.

Finally, one of my friends (another seventy-year-old from Houston) caught up with us. He had hiked these trails several times in the past.

"Hey! Pull over for a minute. Let's catch our breath and give the girls a chance to catch up. They stopped down the trail to take a pee. They found a cave on the side of the cliff."

"Aren't they concerned about the rattlesnakes?" I asked. "Snakes rest in those cool caves during the day."

"Don't tell them about snakes. They'd have pissed their pants rather than have a chance encounter with a den of snakes." He grinned at me.

"Ray, let me tell you how I handle this section of the trail. It's only going to get steeper as we go. What I do is take ten steps and then sit down to catch my breath and admire the scenery; after all, that is why we are here. If we just wanted to hike, we could have done that in Houston."

"Good idea. We'll stay with you the rest of the way out."

The rim was in sight, but we were still some two miles down. The trail is mostly switchbacks near the top. Two miles equates to several hours at 7,000 feet. Leigh was exhausted. She began crying. She couldn't say I hadn't warned her. I had tried everything in my trick book to dissuade her from coming on the trip. She got a lot of sympathy from Lonnie and the girls — but not from me. I was dealing with my own exhaustion. That helicopter didn't seem like a bad idea now.

We made it to the rim just in time to see the sun slip behind the horizon for the second time in two days. Unbelievably, we had made it to the bottom of the canyon and back out in two days. We dragged our ragged butts to our cabin. After a quick shower to wash the red dust from our bodies, we met the others in the big house for dinner. I can't ever remember enjoying a martini as much as I did that one!

Leigh and I left for Phoenix the following morning. Although our muscles burned from the hike, we didn't dwell on the pain too much. We were happy, and sad, to be on our way home. We knew we were going off in separate directions when we left Phoenix — Leigh to Houston, me to Tahlequah. It was a sad parting. We both sensed something amiss.

Divine Timing

My flight was overbooked. I took one of the front seats that faced the back. Two men were already seated across from me and a woman from Chicago sat beside me. A large woman boarded the flight a little late and sat between the two men. She was a talker!

During the course of many trivial conversations, she mentioned she was Cherokee. She had been recording music with the Havasupai Indians, whose reservation is located at the bottom of the Grand Canyon.

I told her I worked for the Cherokees. Not only did she recognize my name but she knew I had lived in Houston. She had sung at the GOP convention in Houston for George Bush Sr. She went on to tell me that Chief Swimmer had told her he knew me. She said he could arrange for her to stay at my house while she was in Houston. She was married and had two children — poor as a church mouse. One of her sons had club feet. She said club feet appeared to be epidemic among the Cherokees. I never did find out why.

One of the two men across from me broke into our conversation. "I am Cherokee. So is my friend here."

They introduced themselves and joined in the conversation. The tall one was a racehorse owner. He lived in Sallisaw, just off I-40 and Hwy 59 in eastern Oklahoma, near Ft. Smith, Arkansas. The other man owned the "Charley's Chicken" chain of restaurants. He lived in Tulsa. The two were returning from a trip to Vegas where they watched the Evander Holyfield vs. Riddick Bowe fight.

"What a coincidence," I thought. "This has to be more than just another chance meeting." Since my NDE, I had come to expect such "coincidental" occurrences. At times, they appeared to me as illusions — just too incredible to be factual.

The horse rancher asked, "Where'd you grow up? I don't recognize your name."

"Fort Supply, Oklahoma. You probably never heard of it. We had a population of three hundred back then, and it's three hundred to this day," I replied.

"Really? I know exactly where Ft. Supply is. I go quail hunting there every year with a friend of mine."

"Oh yeah? What's his name?"

"Bob Drake."

"You're kidding! Bob and I went to school together. Bob was one of my closest friends. I haven't seen him in years. I hear he is one mean man," I said.

The rancher responded, "Bob does not have a mean bone in his body. He can be tough, but he isn't mean."

The woman from Chicago looked at the four of us and asked, "Are you guys all from the same family? Been to a family reunion or something?"

We got a chuckle out of her comment.

"No. We're not directly related, but we're all Cherokee," said the horseman.

She thought that was a hoot. In her mind, Indians should be wearing buckskins, moccasins, and beads.

This was an omen of good things to come. This has happened to me so many times, I recognize an omen when I see one. I made the right choice in moving here. It's divine destiny. God always seems to put me in the right place at the right time. "Does He do this for everyone?" I mused.

Upon my return to Tahlequah toward the end of 1992, my mental health was as good as it had ever been. I felt great. My body felt renewed and my mind fresh. Perhaps the insanity was over — forever.

Ray Loyd Tune

Working for the Indians

We purchased a home in Tahlequah, thirty miles from my office. I couldn't believe this was the house Leigh wanted. The long brown-and-gold shag carpeting, the mustard-yellow walls in the living areas, multi-colored bedrooms with floor-to-ceiling wallpaper, Pepto-Bismol pink bathrooms — what was she thinking?

I began remodeling immediately. I told Leigh to pick out paint colors, new tile for the bathrooms, and wallpaper. That was a big mistake. I didn't like any of it and told her so. I had my own ideas and opinions.

"If you didn't want my opinion, why did you even ask me?" She had disapproval written all over her face.

"What is with her?" I asked myself. "Something's wrong. Doesn't she like the town? Maybe it's the house. No, the house is far larger and nicer than anything we've lived in."

"It must something to do with her friend at the office," I thought.

She called me nearly every evening to tell me she loved me. That was strange. She never told me she loved me when we lived together. Then again, perhaps she actually did miss me — I'd been in Tahlequah for four months. The last time we had seen each other had been in Arizona.

Four months into the new job, Akram, an IT consultant I brought in from Houston invited me to play bingo with several employees. I didn't want to go. It was 6:00 p.m., and cold and damp outside. The board of director's meeting was the following day and I still hadn't completed the financials. Preparation generally required a minimum of three days. Here I was trying to cram it into 24 hours. After some arm twisting, I agreed. "Hell I've got to stop and eat sometime," I thought.

Erma, one of our office workers, said she would ride with Akram. I told them to go on ahead and I would come later in my own car. This would most likely cause me to work throughout the night. Erma was slight of build, pure black hair and fiery brown eyes. She spent more time socializing than working. She had grown up on a small rocky farm with her parents and three sisters. They were dependent on Indian handouts, FDA commodities, and wild plants such as poke salad greens, wild basil, peaches, and plenty of squirrel and deer. In short, they ate well.

It was my first time playing bingo for money. What might have been ecstasy for some was misery for me — three women helping me play. Two games in and I won. Fourth game, I won again. I was up about $150.00. I bought burgers for the table along with fries and soft drinks. That was enough for me. I made a graceful exit and excused myself. "I've got to leave," I said.

Akram said, "We have to go also."

Erma rode there with Akram; she had to leave when he did, but she changed the plans.

"Akram, I'm going to ride back to the plant with Ray. That way you go can directly to Tahlequah without going through Stilwell. Is that okay with you Ray?"

"Sure. Your car is at the plant. That's a good idea," he said.

It was raining heavily and spitting snow now. Erma grabbed my hand and said, "I'm scared of thunderstorms. I can't stand them."

"Don't be afraid. It's okay. Just hang in there."

That she did. All the way to Stilwell.

Erma had grown up in a small Indian home with her parents and three sisters. During slaughtering season, her job was to hold the hog cuts and guide them into a large galvanized washbasin while her father gutted the hogs. It reminded me of Silence of the Lambs. She often spoke of how warm and slimy the guts felt when they flopped out of the hog's frame. She must have told the story a dozen times. In the back of my mind, I knew it still disturbed her. I had been in more than a few slaughterhouses in my life — always steering clear of the paunch line. It was way too grisly for me. It made me queasy just listening to her.

Her mother had had an affair with some man at some point during her marriage. One evening the beau walked through the woods, snuck up to the house and opened fire with a high-powered rifle. The four children were inside. The bullet holes are still visible after all these years. It's no wonder Erma was so odd.

As a teen, she carried a half pint of Wild Turkey inside her boot top — I guess that would make her a "bootlegger." She was born with scoliosis, which affected her walk — she waddled like a duck. Of course, she couldn't see the defect. It was only visible from the back. As a youngster, she was very homely. According to her sisters, she had a violent temper even then —violent as in pulling knives and meat forks when irritated. She didn't give a shit about who was present. When her temper flared, her mind switched from confrontational to homicidal, with no in between. She was, and is today, a ticking time bomb. After all this time, I still read the crime reports to see if she has stabbed someone.

When we arrived at the plant in the pouring rain, I bid her farewell.

"I've got to go back to work. See you tomorrow."

"Can I come in and help you?" she asked.

"No. What I've got to do is something only I can do. That is why they hired me."

"I won't be any problem. I promise. I can make coffee," she pleaded.

"Coffee sounds good. Come on in." I figured she was just a poor Indian kid with nowhere to go except back home with her parents and her two sisters. It wouldn't hurt. She was a distraction, but that was okay. It would force me to concentrate.

There was an over-overstuffed sofa in my office. I'd take naps on it at noon and sometimes at night. It was not unusual for me to work until three in the morning. Erma made coffee and sat on the sofa until well after midnight. Finally, she got up to leave. She walked behind my chair and gave me a big hug.

"Thanks for allowing me to stay. I had a good time."

She left, leaving me with a shit pot full of work.

"Hmmm, I kind of wished she'd have stayed," I thought. God knows, I could have used some companionship. "Oh well. It's for the better."

Next day she strolled into my office as if she had known me all her life. She asked me, "What are you doing tonight?"

"Working, as usual," I answered.

"Want to go somewhere?" she asked.

"No. Thanks for asking though."

She continued to stand there looking at me.

"Uh-oh. She wants something more than companionship," I thought.

I always left my office door open, except when I was napping or on the phone with my boss or a client, eliminating suspicion from imaginative minds. Here she was, asking me out. My door was wide open.

"Erma, I am married with two children. Going out with a single woman might be taken wrong."

Spurned, she walked out. Sure enough, the CEO's secretary (very much the busybody) called the marketing manager, Meredith and asked for a meeting. Meredith came to the secretary's desk, just outside my office. I couldn't hear everything they were saying, but enough to know they were talking about Erma.

Erma was shameless in her pursuit. I knew better than to take her anywhere without a chaperone. One evening I invited a friend to dinner. Rufus, also from Houston who was doing some consulting work for me. Erma invited herself along. We went to a popular restaurant on the Illinois River. There was a waiting line, as usual, so we sat on the veranda until our table was ready. It was a quiet evening, just about dusk. Stars sprinkled the otherwise clear sky.

We ordered steaks. Erma had never in her life used a knife to cut her food. She tried in vain to cut her steak with a fork. Both of us felt sorry for her. Rufus said: "Let me cut your steak for you." It was embarrassing for Rufus and me, but it didn't seem to bother her. I suspect she would have been more comfortable eating with her fingers

From sympathy, to friendship, and on to an illicit relationship, all within six months of my arrival. I'd been sober for two years. She was a drinker — and a sorry one at that. Two drinks and she became wild-eyed and zany. Definitely a gal to avoid.

Walking into Temptation

Each May, I hiked the Talimena Scenic Drive on Oklahoma Highway 1 in the Kiamichi Mountains. It has a spectacular view, but it's a grueling hike. The grade is twenty degrees in places — as a matter of fact, in most places. Now that I lived in Oklahoma, I felt compelled to make the pilgrimage. May 1993 the countryside was ablaze with colors of red, blue, green and violet. The hike up, as a rule, took half a day. The trek begs for companionship — someone to share the beauty. I invited Meredith, our marketing manager, and Erma — ever so mindful as to not be alone with Erma.

The weekend of the trip rolled around. Meredith backed out — leaving only Erma and myself. Although I knew better, I took Erma with me just the same. Ninety percent of the employees at Cherokee Nation Industries were women. I couldn't walk through the plant without starting a rumor. Their tongues would wag for an hour about how I spent more time talking to one employee than to another. I knew the hiking trip with Erma could provide enough fodder to keep the rumor mill going for days — and it did.

We made the trip just the same. The first day was a blast. She was an adept hiker, never talking too much, and never lagging behind. We'd had such a good time together, we decided to stay over that night and return to the mountain the next day. Damn big mistake. She was to sleep on the sofa and I on the bed. Sometime during the night, passion took over.

The next day, we were somewhat ashamed of our behavior from the previous night. We didn't talk much — guilt filled my gut. After a day of silence and introspection, we returned to Stilwell. It was a quiet trip — almost too quiet. All I could hear were the voices of my wife and children. Every now and again, a passing truck interrupted the voices.

Come Monday evening, the whole damn town was abuzz with talk of our relationship. Lesson learned. It's virtually impossible to talk your way out of something you acted yourself into. There was no way to extricate my own culpability with fellow employees. One after another, the older women told me how shameful my conduct was.

With our secret out, I thought, "What the hell? I've nothing to lose. Why not continue?" And we did. Thus began a long stream of weekend meetings. I couldn't have gotten rid of Erma after that, even if I had wanted to.

Love Triangle

Here I was, stuck with a starry-eyed girl who had the hots for me and had become accustomed to the finer things in life. Naturally, that's when Leigh and the children moved to Tahlequah. During Leigh's and my separation, she had gained forty pounds. She had gone from a size 8 to a 16 in just a little over seven months. Erma was a petite size 4. Leigh was educated, well-mannered and even-tempered. Erma was poorly educated, a social abnormality and ill-tempered. They were polar opposites. I loved Leigh, despite her obesity. I tolerated Erma.

Beyond a doubt, I had to quit my executive position with the Cherokee Nation. My relationship with Erma was too much for the company to cope with. Again, I made the preemptive strike. I began looking for other employment.

Here I was with a new home and what I thought was to be a new beginning. I had uprooted my family and planted them in a very strange environment — no friends, no relatives. Just the four of us. But my old ways continued.

"'Wherever I go, I am there! I surrender. I can no more change my behavior than I can stop breathing," I chastised myself. What a piece of dog crap I had become. The serenity I'd hoped to find in Tahlequah was short-lived. I was not suicidal, but I did have a huge empty pit in my stomach.

I cranked up the résumé mill yet again, as I had so many times over the years. With an MBA, I seldom had difficulty finding employment. My problem was me; I couldn't cope with success. I'd put my family through so much grief I could never forgive myself. "Love oneself" was but another hollow expression beyond my comprehension.

Chief Wilma Mankiller

Leigh and I were walking through the Wal-Mart parking lot in Tahlequah one summer day when a familiar voice rang out from a nearby station wagon. "Excuse me sir! Would you remove the cap off my coke bottle?"

It was Chief Wilma Mankiller, leader of the Cherokee Nation. Since she didn't call me by name, I assumed she didn't remember me — although she attended all of my board meetings. The following evening, the comptroller of the Tribe called me:

"Ray, my name is Charles Thompson. I am comptroller for the tribe. We have met several times at board meetings. The Chief asked me to call you about a job. We purchased a new software package and an IBM computer to run it on two years ago, and it's still not working. We paid over $500,000. She wants it installed and she thinks you are the man to get it done. What do you say?"

"I don't know what to say. The project sounds a bit over my head. Let me think about for a while."

"Don't take too long. You know Wilma, she is not all that patient," he said.

After some consideration, I decided it was not for me. I didn't bother calling Charles back. That evening, the Chief called. "Ray, we really need your help. Please, at least come in and talk with our accounting people. You can begin whenever you want, as long as it's this week. Talk to Charles about compensation. We'll most likely start you as a consultant."

A consultant, huh? Right up my alley. I love consulting. I could work my own hours. Consultants are paid by the hour. Besides, I can't say no to Wilma. She is just too charismatic, I rationalized.

Filled with hubris, I agreed to take the job. I started work the same day. Money was great. Unlimited hours. And away I go — again. At this point in my life, I had experienced that mental rush so many times that I knew what was to follow. First would come the surge of elation, then I'd get cocky and do something brainless to sabotage my good fortune.

Erma began coming to our house in Tahlequah. When we wouldn't let her in, she'd sit on our front porch, whining like a forlorn puppy that had just lost its mother. One day I let her come in to get a drink and lie down in my son's room. She sobbed the entire time. I went to her side, trying to calm her. I was always a sucker for the crying thing.

My wife said, "It's an act, Ray. I do know when a woman is trying to con you. And she is putting on one damn good performance."

In retrospect, I realize Erma only wanted access to our home to sprinkle some witch medicine around. She, and her family at large, believed in and used Indian remedies. Want to look attractive to someone? Go to the forest. Look for a leaf with some water in the curl. Wipe the water on your face, and presto, you are Cinderella. Want to bring harm to a nemesis? Get some "medicine" from a shaman and use it according to directions. The "medicine man" conjures magic over; tobacco leaves, cigarettes, soap, feathers and medicine balls, you name it they conjure over it. And yes, one is expected to pay for the concoction. I am quite sure Erma still uses it. It's difficult to remove the stripes from a tiger.

My illicit behavior was indefensible — and I knew it. Primarily to extract myself from the quagmire, I took a consulting job in San Francisco in the summer of '95, leaving Leigh in charge of the consulting job at the tribe.

Medicine Man Magic

Erma rode with me on one of my trips to the Bay Area. She had arranged a visit with Tony, a widely popular medicine man. He lived in Okarche, Oklahoma, just off I-40. It was on the way, so I didn't mind the stop. People from all over the United States called on Tony for various cures. One man flew him to Nebraska to cure his cancer. A business owner called him to Tulsa to rid his company of spirits — the company was nearing bankruptcy. Many locals dropped by his house regularly just for a preemptive dose of medicine.

Tony lived in Hughes County. You have to know the area to find his house. He lived in Indian housing, but his was a nice brick home, not the shanties one normally sees. We arrived about 10:00 a.m. Tony had prepared a gallon of potion for me — none for Erma.

"This is a special medicine," he said. "I waited until everything was just right to make it. I make it from spring water and the roots of a red willow tree. It has to be prepared at night. There can't be any clouds in the sky for the following 24 hours. If the clouds come up, I've got to start all over again. Go to my bedroom and drink the entire gallon. There's a washbasin on the floor. That's for throwing up in. You'll throw up most of the water. I can tell from the vomit what we need to do next." Erma said Tony's medicine would ensure us a safe trip to California and success with my consulting job. I thought, "What the shit. It can't hurt anything."

After waiting about an hour, I said, "Guess it's not going to work for me. We have to get back on the road. Thanks just the same."

I handed him $50.00 and we hit the road. We drove all day, arriving in Tucumcari, New Mexico, around 8:00 that evening. We rented a motel room so we could clean the road grime from our bodies and get a little sleep before forging on to San Francisco.

Late in the night, I awoke in a puddle of sweat. I never threw up but, mystically, I purged the water through my sweat glands. That was a shocker. I never found out what the medicine was designed to do. Since Erma arranged the meeting, I assumed it had more to do with her than me.

I got an apartment in San Francisco. Erma later moved there to be with me. She was quite the distraction. The owner of the company knew my wife and took offense at my relationship with Erma. I sensed the outcome, this was to be a very short-term assignment. In the interim, between realizing my future fate and working, I continued my job as a cost-reduction consultant.

One project was to reduce insurance costs. The owner of an insurance company bidding on a new contract invited me to lunch with some of his associates. Glad to get a free meal, I readily accepted. I climbed into the back of his dated Cadillac. There was an older man already sitting there. I introduced myself. He reciprocated, "I'm Y.A. Tittle."

The name didn't set off any bells in my head. Off to lunch we went. The group was amazed that I was not ecstatic about meeting Y.A. Finally, one of the younger men said, "Dad was a professional football player. He played with the Giants, Colts, and later here in San Francisco with the 49ers."

Still no bells went off. Then the old gent told me his story. He had grown up in Marshall, Texas, where he was a star player on the local football team. He went on to play for Texas and later LSU. During his professional days, Y.A. played for the Colts, 49ers, and the Giants. I still didn't recognize the name, but I did know about Marshall, Texas. We talked about Marshall for thirty minutes. Then his son rudely broke into our conversation. "Dad, we're here to talk about insurance. Can you and Ray continue your conversation some other time?"

That pissed me off and I let him know it. Before the extended lunch was over, Y.A. invited me to spend a week at his places in Marshall, Sedona, Arizona, and Jamaica. We became good friends. And yes, Y.A.'s son did write the insurance contract for my client.

Peering into the Future

Erma and I spent our weekends walking the piers and taking short trips to Alcatraz, the Presidio, and of course the Golden Gate Bridge. One Sunday, we went to the long pier across the road from Pacifica. Sometime after dark, we returned to our apartment. Later that evening she discovered her ring - an inexpensive friendship ring I had purchased from a pawnshop in McAlester, Oklahoma - was missing. She insisted I go back to the pier and find it.

"Are you crazy? It's dark outside. You can't find it in the dark."

"Well, I'll go by myself then," she cried.

"Erma, if you will wait until tomorrow, I'll take you back to the pier at daybreak. We can look until 7:30. I've got to be at work by 8:00." She was very unhappy with my offer, but agreed.

The next morning she woke me at 6:00. We drove over the mountain to Pacifica. We split up. She walked on the right side of the pier — I on the left. We searched every square foot by traversing back and forth to the center and then back to the railing. At long last, we came to the end of the pier's extension into the Pacific. She continued on an offshoot by herself.

I stood at the end, watching a gathering of gulls pick the meat from the carcasses of some rotting rockfish. A precognition came over me like a blanket. I couldn't take my eyes off the birds. I looked down amidst the flock and there in plain sight was her ring. I picked it up and waited for her to return. Her eyes were welling up, ready to flood tears.

"Hold out your hand Erma. Now close your eyes and try to envision your ring." I placed the ring on her finger. She became hysterical with joy.

Looking back, I don't recall ever having paranormal abilities prior to my NDE in 1969. After the NDE, precognition was an integral part of my life — and success. It was as much a part of my life as eating, drinking and breathing. I came to rely on it in my day-to-day activities. It wasn't even a conscious effort.

Erma thought I had Indian "magic." My psychic abilities became a parlor game for her personal enjoyment — something I find very unpleasant, even to this day. But it's true. I can see some events far into the future. Other times I see occurrences that are just around the corner.

Over the years, I've discovered, like Edgar Cayce, that our powers cannot be used for personal aggrandizement. I can, and do, predict stock prices (and the timing thereof) for my good friends, but not for my own gain. Each time I've tried to use my gift for selfish purposes, I end up losing my ass. I've never tried healing anyone. I don't know if it would work or not. When a friend becomes deathly ill, I use prayer. Maybe prayer is a form of psychic healing.

Another Lost Love

The trip home from San Francisco was exciting. We had Oklahoma license plates and were pulling a U-Haul trailer. We parked the trailer at an airport parking lot about thirty miles north of Sedona, and went on to Sedona. Little did we realize the FBI was searching for Timothy McVeigh's accomplices. They suspected the villains lived near Kingston, close to where we left the trailer. What a stir that created. Oklahoma tags, a parked trailer and, worse yet, at an airport.

When we got back to Oklahoma, I moved back in with Leigh and took over the consulting project again. By now, Leigh knew about my relationship with Erma. She was furious, as one might imagine. I didn't (and couldn't) deny it.

Leigh continued to get calls from her male friend in Houston. One weekend she informed me she was going to Houston for a few days to visit her friends. Having used that excuse myself, I knew exactly what was in the offing. I can't say that I blamed her — but it did cut deeply.

Six months later, at the beginning of 1996, my wife and I had seven employees and we were making a good living as consultants. Then the tribe got a new controller who wanted to stop all work on the software installation. The controller was later charged with embezzling funds stolen from deposits. To this day, I think she terminated our contract for fear we might discover the missing deposits.

Embezzlement was common at the tribe. Over the past several years, three other women had been charged with the same thing. Could it be that the men just don't get caught?

Leigh finally gave up, or gave out. My long history of infidelity caught up with me. We separated. She found another lover. I moved in with Erma. I lost a wonderful wife, lover and friend — as I had twice before.

"Why? Why? Why?" I asked myself. "I've given up everything for nothing." It was clear that whatever was eating at my brain had one hell of an appetite.

The Tribe hired Leigh full-time to complete the software conversion. The Cherokee Tribe is and has always been a matriarchal society. In fact, any Cherokee woman who has the least bit of integrity can find life-long employment with the tribe. Sixteen years later, she is now operations director for the IT department. Not bad for a woman with no self-confidence — at least, not while we were married. Then again, who could have had self-confidence after living in my shadow for seventeen years? I am so proud of her.

Divorce Déjà vu

After Leigh left me, I received three employment offers within a month, opting for a consulting position in Wichita Falls, Texas. It gave me the opportunity to see if the company was a good fit, and gave the company a chance to see my performance.

The CEO offered me vice-presidency of manufacturing within ninety days. Erma had moved to Wichita Falls with me. She found work, and I had landed a dream job. Back on a pink cloud! I was exuberant — such elation is difficult to mask. I "rocked!" Bring out the Jack Daniels.

Carol, a youthful investment banker from Connecticut, owned the company. Some employees didn't care for her. As for me, I loved her. She was a very astute businessperson. Later, I found that her genuine interest was to flip the company but she had been unable to find a suitable buyer. She gave me carte blanche authority to mold the factory into what I envisioned. The company CEO and I teamed well. As a matter of fact, I teamed well with everyone at the company.

Finally, a serious player who heard about our progressive manufacturing philosophy made a serious offer. Carol had purchased the company for $7 million several years prior to my arrival. She'd had a few nibbles, but no serious buyers, mostly tire kickers whose real motive was to see the company's financial records.

Carol and our CEO asked me to attend the subsequent "due diligence" meetings. I had designed and implemented the manufacturing philosophy so I had to be the one to make the sale. To make a long story short, she sold the company for $24 million. Carol masterfully pulled off the sale of the year, if not of the decade. She made 300% within seven years. Not too shabby for a young woman with two teenage girls.

The ink had no sooner dried when the new management began looking for ways to cut overhead. They were less than pleased with my salary — it stuck out like a whore in church. I was low-hanging fruit to them. Their plans were to replace me and the other executive staff members with loyal soldiers from their mother company. It took them less than ninety days to implement their plan.

Then Erma began her shit again. One evening, for no reason, she slung a wine glass across the room at me, painting burgundy on the walls and carpeting and hitting me. That was not enough; she punched me in the nose — nearly knocking me to my knees. Then she dug her long, dirty nails into the side of my face, leaving a six-inch scar. This time I defended myself, showing her what it felt like to be abused.

While I was at work the next day, she called my brother who had been sober for over twenty years. She concocted a story of how I beat her. Still playing God after twenty years of AA, he refused to call and validate her story. His advice was for her to move everything — everything— out of my house, including my gun collection, furnishings, and cars, and move back to Oklahoma.

I came home to an empty house.

Later in the week, she called and told me she was sleeping in her rental truck with a car trailer in tow, parked along the curb of a residential neighborhood.

"Can I come home? I don't have the money for an apartment."

Kind of a sad story for a woman who walked away from a household income in excess of $130K per year.

"Why did you leave in the first place?" I asked.

"Your brother told me to."

"Call him. If it was his idea, I'm sure he would be happy to let you move in with him."

Her mother called me later and asked why I had abused her daughter.

"Is that what she told you?"

"Yes she did. She also said you called and begged her to return."

"Louise, how could I have called her? She doesn't have a phone. She called me from a pay phone and told me she was living out of a truck."

"She didn't tell me about that," Louise said.

Erma poisoned the water wells. She had taken my brother's advice about moving out, now here she was asking to come back home. She'd lied to her mother, and she'd lied about me abusing her. She knocked out three allies in one broad stroke.

Nevertheless, I let her return — at her own expense. She also had to unload the truck and place all the furniture back where it belonged. The following day, upon returning from work, I found the two cars back in the driveway, and all the furniture and the wall hangings in place, just as if nothing had ever happened. I've no idea how she unloaded the truck.

She had not been back two months when she picked me up at the hospital where I had received ten stitches after falling from the top of a building. On the way home, she was driving down a busy street in front of the country club — cars on both sides and two behind us — when she slugged me in the side of my head. Even though she was driving, she hit me hard enough to bang my head against the passenger side window. To this day, I don't know why she did it. Too bad my brother wasn't nearby, he would have enjoyed it.

A Hop, Skip, and Jump

Spring, 1999. Again, I was out of a job. I put out my feelers, and waited for the next offer. Within two weeks, I received two invitations to interview — both in Oklahoma. Both companies had revenues in excess of $130 million. I took the one in Tulsa. Subsequently, they asked me to work at their plant in Longview, Texas. Longview is a beautiful city. I had wanted to live and work in Longview since graduating from college. I moved into a motel until I could find a house.

On a weekend visit to Longview, Erma went into one of her many hysterical manic fits and left in a rage. This was the evening of May 12th. The next day a detective called my motel room looking for her. I figured she had done something the night before to someone who wouldn't put up with her crap. As it turned out, they had spent the night together, or so she said.

Somewhere, sometime, somehow Erma got pregnant. She was a nut case to begin with. Now that her hormones were roaring, she became totally out of control. According to her doctor, May 12th was when she got pregnant. I had not slept with her for over a week. So who had?

She needed insurance for the baby, so we agreed to marry — for insurance alone. I drew up prenuptials, knowing that she would at some point want a divorce and a piece of my real estate. The same way I had suspected Leigh's relationship with her boy in Houston, I thought the unborn child was not of my making.

Erma gave birth to a beautiful little boy in March of 2000. I was 57 — she 24. With the aid of the insurance provided by my company, most of her hospital expenses were paid.

The work was fine. The pay was great. But the management team and organizational structure were dysfunctional, to say the least. A year after I began working for this company, I was on my way back to Houston. The business I had launched in 1985 wanted me to return as

CEO and president. It had changed ownership twice since my departure. The new owner offered me a piece of the pie if and when the company sold. Within two quarters, I gave him the first profit the company had made in five years — earning $250 thousand in one month alone.

The owner, an old man from Alabama, and the COO were both paranoid morons. Their combined IQ didn't exceed 130. They were so full of themselves they stunk like shit. The younger claimed to be the "Mozart" of the machining industry; the older one acted as if he was the Warren Buffet of industry. My plan was to stay just long enough to collect my fee. The time looked ripe to sell but the old man was asking $6 million, no one in his right mind would have purchased the company at that price. My own evaluation was $3 million - tops. Two companies entered due diligence with us at about the same time. Independently, they valued the company at $3 million. My valuation was spot on. However, neither of the two actually made an offer. In retrospect, I think they sensed the same dysfunctional organization I had. What is a company without its employees — sane employees, that is?

In less than a year, the three of us were so distrustful of one another, I left.

The Final Straw

Erma and I were now stuck with one another. I owned three homes in Houston: two from my marriage with Leigh, and now the one with Erma. This house was a large one. I couldn't sell it, so I added it to my rental property inventory.

At 58, I was through with the corporate world and was ready to semi-retire. We moved back to Oklahoma, where my wife and son could receive 100% free medical benefits through the Bureau of Indian Affairs. I set up a small company, mining landscaping stones from the local mountains. I went deeply in debt to purchase heavy equipment for the business.

It was June of 2001 and I had not taken a drink for over three years. My weight and stamina were back to my high school days, and my mania seemed to me to be in check. It took about a year to find another large house. The one we found turned out to be excessively large for the three of us. Everything was starting to fall into place so, just as expected, it all fell apart.

Erma went totally berserk. First, she began having one affair after another. I had remained loyal to her, but I just couldn't bring myself to love her. She had the disposition of a pit bull — throwing objects, tearing doors off kitchen cabinets, and kicking in doors. I could have (and should have) filed charges for "domestic abuse against a senior in the presence of a minor" — her son. For fear of tarnishing my name in her small hometown of Stilwell, I didn't.

Then one day she packed her overnight bag, took the boy and my car, and left. I didn't hear from her for three days. When she finally called, she wanted to return home. "No. You no longer have a home. Stay where you are," I told her.

One afternoon she crawled over the fence and began rifling my house. I called the police this time. She thought they would side with her. However, after she pulled out a butcher knife, a huge officer pulled his service pistol and told her to put the knife down. She did and they escorted her back to her car with her two Wal-Mart plastic bags of purloined plates, cups and silverware.

Like so many times before, she called after she'd cooled down, wanting to return home.

"You should have thought about a home before you abandoned this one."

"I didn't abandon you. I just wanted some time by myself," she said.

"Sorry. Fool me once, shame on you. Fool me twice, shame on me. Your time has come and gone. Shame on me. There won't be a third."

She filed for divorce. She was the single biggest mistake of my life. In retrospect, she was nothing but a shrewd con — out to skin a well-to-do older man. She wrangled a meager amount of money from me but mostly got some gaudy baubles, bangles, and beads. I kept the homes in Houston and Oklahoma.

I believe monogamy is not a natural state of being, at least not for me. We are, by nature, here to procreate. It's matter of keeping our species from going extinct. "Spread that seed to the wind."

Peace at Last

Losing Erma was like losing a millstone. Damn, it felt good to be rid of her. It felt even better to have a court order enforcing the split. She could no longer come into my house at random. Again, my mind became stable. Sanity began to blossom.

I often sat on the back porch admiring the wildlife. The house had an orchard in the back, mostly apple, cherry and peach trees. Deer came in each evening to lick a salt block I had placed on an old tree stump near the house. A mother skunk paraded through the yard with her six babies as if she owned the place. There were birds of all species eating from my fruit trees on a regular basis. They became so dependent on food from the trees, that when the fruit disappeared, I had to throw birdseed around the base of the trees to keep them from starving.

Two months after Erma left, someone tried to burn my house down. I had been out of town that particular day. I just happened to return home before the flames ate through the ceiling. Fortunately, my insurance covered the damages. I used the proceeds to remodel the entire house — new carpeting, new paint, drapes, and appliances. I changed the locks on the house, and installed safety locks on the windows. That really pissed her off. That was the last time she entered my house.

When I first moved to Stilwell, friends told me that you could have someone killed for a six-pack of beer — I believed them. It crossed my mind more than once that, as crazy as she was, she just might try. By 2004, however, I had as many friends in town as she. I had developed a good reputation, something that took me only four years to do and that she couldn't do in forty.

And so ended my fourth marriage. Mentally, my life was back to normal, if there is such a thing for those of us with mental disorders. However, physically, I was suffering. The stress of the marriage wracked my body. Within the year, I had a heart attack. Just when I thought my health couldn't get any worse, I developed something called polymyalgia rheumatica — some badass stuff. The treatment is much worse than the disease. I lived on prednisone, a form of steroid, for twenty-two months. The side effects of the prednisone were cataracts, osteopenia, diabetes, and blackouts. Blackouts led to concussions, a broken ankle, and fractured ribs, which in turn punctured a lung. It made me wonder if Erma had found a way to sneak some Indian medicine into my house.

I would like to say, "Everyone lived happy ever after." I'd like to, but I can't. As I mentioned earlier, "Wherever I go, I am there." With Erma out of my life, there was no one left to blame. Lord knows I could have used a scapegoat many times post divorce.

Pathological Impulsiveness

Compared to most people, my life and decisions had always been pedal-to-the-floor. For example, I love Mercedes Benz automobiles. When married, I had two, one for Erma and one for me. I lost one in the divorce. I just had to have another. My favorite pastime is to watch car sales on eBay. Being an impulsive type of individual, I purchased another Benz from a seller in New Jersey. This car was a black beauty. It had one minor glitch — the electric switch for the back window didn't operate. I have the patience of a deer with its antlers stuck in a barbed wire fence. I took the car to a friend of mine to have the switch repaired. His shop was seven miles off the highway, down a chunky gravel road. He was too busy to repair the car at the time, so I left it with him.

A week later and he still had not repaired it. I got pissed and picked it up. Still mad, I cranked my beauty up to about 70 on the rocky road. Ahead of me, I saw a pile of rock in my lane. I slammed on the brakes. The front of the car bowed down as if it was greeting the queen. The bottom of the engine acted like a shovel — scooping up the pile of rocks and thrusting them into the oil pan. Within minutes the engine froze. Yeah, I learned a bit about humility. I had to call my friend to tow my car back to his shop. He laughed his ass off. He was kind enough to offer me $350 for my now disabled Benz, which pissed me off even more. What an insult.

I figured, "I'll show that prick." I bought a new engine and had a local shop install it. The locals did an okay job with the installation, but ruined the transmission in the process. By now I had too much pride and money invested to turn back. I hauled it to a Mercedes shop in Fayetteville, Arkansas. They rebuilt the tranny. I didn't mind paying them for their services, but I sure hated listening to their shit about how badly I had screwed up in taking the car to a non-Mercedes shop to begin with.

After all this, I still was not satisfied with the performance of the car — but I damn sure was not going to tell anyone. Back on eBay I found another Benz in Austin,

Texas. Same make. Same model year. Less mileage. It did need a paint job. My son and I went to Austin and drove the new one back to Stilwell. It ran like a new car. Again, I spent several thousand dollars on repairs and a paint job. It looked like a new car. It looked so good I listed it on eBay and sold it within three days of the listing. Why? Beats the shit out of me. I guess so I could go buy another.

Less than a month after selling the new one, my black money-pit began having transmission problems again. By now, I was tired of pouring cash into it. So I sold it as-is on eBay for pennies on the dollar. Today, I am back on eBay, looking for the next good deal. Does that sound a bit like insanity?

Training for Risk

Medical professionals state that one characteristic of bipolar disorder is the "tendency to engage in behavior that could have serious consequences, such as spending." Reckless behavior in general might be construed as signs of a disorder, such as risky investments and obsessive chance-taking. If that is a true assessment, then I am bipolar.

I acquired my love of risky activities the old-fashioned way, from my stepfather. During my high school days, he became a cattle trader, buying cattle one week and selling them the next. It was so much an addiction for him that he mortgaged a farm and purchased his own livestock auction. One week he would be up by $20K, the next down by $30K. Mother never knew when she had discretionary money, so she played it safe by scrimping on everything.

The addiction became so powerful that he began paying a 10% finder's commission to people who would "spot deals" for him. When you are buying a herd of cattle, 10% can amount to more than the profit potential. I chauffeured him to various auctions and ranches every chance I got. I loved to drive and he liked sleeping between trades. One day I saw him write a check to a "spotter" for $3,600 (this was in the sixties). This was equivalent to mother's grocery budget for the year. From that day on, I was hooked.

Having learned the art of trading at my stepfather's side, I began making my own deals. On auction days, I worked at our sale-barn as a cattle "packager", in other words I separated cattle by sex, color, and age so as to make the package more marketable. I was the last person to see the cattle prior to them entering the auction arena. I'd find a nervous rancher, anxious to dump a few head so as not to take a loss in the ring, and purchase them from him. If I didn't make money on the deal, I'd put the cattle in a pen and feed them until the next auction. The feed didn't cost me anything, nor were there any auction fees — just pure profit. God I love capitalism.

His profligacy got him in a financial bind at one point. He had sold a herd of cattle in an auction that he had just purchased. Only one problem with that transaction was that he hadn't paid the rancher for the cattle yet. Two days later, the FBI arrested him at a crap table in Las Vegas, where he had lost the $20,000, but then had won it back and even had a slim profit. He got to spend a few weeks in jail. The net result of that transaction was he now had to sell the mortgaged farm, a ranch, all the cattle and his beloved auction house.

Back to earth, like a mortal, he started over, like any other individual would do. However, he was not like any other individual. Within a year, he was back in the cattle-trading arena. This time around, he learned the cattle feeding industry, at which he excelled. The feeding business involved buying large lots of cattle, feeding them for a period and then reselling the fattened herd to large processing plants. The industry also exposed traders to the commodity market, which was like pouring gasoline on a fire when it came to my stepfather, it was just his cup of tea - or was it scotch? By and by, he lost his fortune again and had to start over, for the third or fourth time.

This time around, he found a feed yard that was in foreclosure. Prudential held the mortgage on the operation, but knew nothing about running it. They just wanted to get rid of it. He made them an offer. "I'll take it off your hands if you will give me all the assets," which amounted to a little over a hundred thousand dollars. Unbelievably, they accepted his offer. He was out a total of $450.00. He did have to pay Prudential a small percent of the profits, until such time they had recouped their book value.

Three years later and he had three feed operations. All of this from a $450 investment. Through his large network of cattle traders, feeders and ranchers, he built each of them up to the point where Beatrice Food offered to buy him out. Even though he didn't pay anything for them, he sold out too cheaply, realizing a little under a million for the three.

A million dollars was not that big of a deal to him, but it sure as hell was to my mother. For the first time in her fifty years of life, she felt financially secure. Mother died four years later. My stepfather continued his risky investments, buying several ranches in western Oklahoma, and raising and training racehorses. Within ten years, he had lost everything, again. This time he was not to recover. Eventually he found a woman in New Mexico who owned thousands of acres of ranch land near the national forest to take him in as a lover. Evelyn made him walk the line. He lived to be 78.

Risk taking is so deeply etched in my psyche that it's a normal way of life. By the time I was 26; I had lost $3,000 in the cattle futures market, purchased five houses, and had run for a public office.

Comparative corporate analysis was my forte in graduate school. With knowledge gleaned from my analytical skill plus my propensity for risk, I found many investments in which to venture money. I love the adrenalin rush from the chance-taking. My sixth sense played a major role in selecting market segments to research. Sometime after my near-death experience, I discovered I had acquired a valuable tool — precognition.

The Great Recession of 2008-2009 provided a glut of opportunities. I was like a kid in a candy store. Stocks were diving everywhere — the only question was which one to buy first. I fell back on my education, did my research, developed an entry and exit strategy, and jumped in with both feet. Even during my soybean trading days, I had a knack for knowing what to buy and when to buy it. Equally important, I knew when to sell. Some say I was just lucky. I think it was a case of chance favoring a prepared mind, plus some premonitions.

My success rate in selecting stocks average 70% (statistically speaking, 51% is considered to be beyond chance).

I said I had an entry and exit strategy. Entry strategy is based on chart analysis; I use head and shoulder formations to predict bottoms and trends. My sell strategy is simple: 30% profit. It does not take a theoretical physicist to see that 70% of my trades exceeded 30%. However, I lost money on every option trade — without exception. Lesson learned. My mind can't crunch numbers and execute trades as fast as a super computer. My advice? Stay away from options unless you are an expert trader.

Final Transformation

It wasn't until I was sixty-six that a psychiatrist diagnosed me as having bipolar disorder. And all this time I thought I just "danced to a different drummer." Doctors had given up on me. Now a psychiatrist tells me I am not manic depressive; I am Bipolar. The only change I've seen is the medication they give me. Lithium is no longer in vogue — that is for manic-depressive personalities. Bipolars get their own drug. The meds do tend to stabilize my moods — but, then again, so does good whiskey.

Medical professionals contend my "thinking" is flawed. The key word(s) that prompted my primary care physician to refer me to a psychiatrist: "Death is of no concern to me." Death is of no concern! Once you graduate from a near-death experience, you no longer fear death. You are much more concerned about living. Death is as certain as birth. No one is getting out of this world alive. Death is very welcoming, actually. To paraphrase cosmologist Stephen Hawking, "...anyone afraid of dying is also probably afraid of the dark." During my sixty-six years on earth, I've only read of one person who did not report the near-death experience as being pleasant and comforting. This one person said she saw images of evil and demons. This is one of hundreds of reported NDEs. How I appear to doctors, or anyone else for that matter, is of little concern to me. Death is but another phase of life. Life is inconsequential; birth is a chance occurrence; death is certain.

The soothing emotions one feels during and after a near-death experience may have some scientific basis. A research team in Ontario was able to stimulate what they call the "God" cell of the right temporal lobe. The subject sensed the presence of five separate entities in the room with her while, of course, she was locked inside a vault, alone. [Morgan Freeman: Through the Wormhole.]

The Diagnosis

A diagnosis of bipolar disorder, Type I, seems to me to be anecdotal. Be honest, how can a medical professional possibly make a diagnosis with a 45-minute interview? Let's examine the facts.

There were a number of extremely rocky times over the years, but I can't remember a single time when I considered suicide. If I ever experienced "depression," it was well disguised and very short-lived. I've felt alone, but never lonesome. But mania had become such a part of my life, I couldn't live without it—it was like living on "speed." I'd buy a house on the spur of the moment, and sell it just as quickly. The same thing with businesses and raw land. The more risky the transaction, the more my adrenalin surged.

Professionals cannot determine what causes bipolar disorder. This means their diagnosis is subjective. Is bipolar the result of a chemical imbalance? If so, surely it can be detected by way of a common blood/chemical analysis. If it's caused by environmental factors, what are the triggers? Perhaps it's hereditary. If so, will DNA analysis detect it? Or is it societally caused?

"Looking back now, I was drunk on power...and alcohol." Sir Winston Churchill

Heredity or Environment?

Heredity, environment and learned behavior are the choices professionals ponder regarding the origins of bipolar disorder.

There are seven children in my family, four from my biological father and three from my stepfather. Of the older four, three are alcoholics, one of whom has been in recovery for thirty years. There are two alcoholics in the family from my stepfather, both in recovery for years. There are two females in the family, neither of whom were alcoholics, but the younger of the two has been in Al-Anon in excess of thirty years. One of her daughters is alcoholic, but has been in recovery for over twenty years.

Three of the older siblings graduated from college, two with advanced degrees. Two of the younger children have bachelor degrees, one in engineering and the other in business. Two boys are highly successful, both with a net worth in excess of $500 thousand. One has a degree and the other does not. Both boys have had emotional issues in the past, most likely associated with heavy drinking, but growing up with our father had to play some role in it.

Two of us from the first family are bipolar, one (myself) confirmed and the other in denial. Both of us have at least one child who has, or had, emotional disorders.

I have five children by three wives. The first two children are now forty-something. Their mother is sound of mind in all respects, as were her parents. My oldest, a boy, was 100 % manic (he was the one booted out of Montessori school in Aspen) until puberty. He was born with severe allergies. His system reacted vehemently to grains, cow's milk, and red ant bites. We had many wild excursions at the emergency room with him and his doctor. At puberty, he made a 180-degree turn and became docile, non-confrontational, sociable, loving, and caring, as he remains today. Unlike his father, he never fell for the drug scene, but did like his beer.

His sister, on the other hand, was born with mania. It only grew worse with age. By the time she was a teen, she was unmanageable. She can be sweet and loving when she wants to be, or when she has to be; her natural state is to flash over at the slightest provocation. She is now married. The marriage and subsequent birth of a child has helped stabilize her mood swings. I hope her son will be just abrasive enough to polish her tough skin — then they'll both be diamonds.

The next set of children also had a sane mother and grandparents. Both children are now in their thirties; one has completed his degree and my daughter is still pursuing hers. Neither have children. I can't tell whether my son is more addicted to food or beer. He is an excellent chef, and a fair drinker. My daughter is just a good cook. Both are very stable, well rounded and industrious.

The youngest boy is now eleven. I love him just as much as if he was my own. He is sociable, participates in school sports, and shows no signs of mania or depression. If I am manic, his mother is MANIC in bold, being violent, irrational, quick to flare, and both emotionally and physically abusive.

The only common factor shared by my children is their father. I was not physically abusive, but my habitual absence surely constituted emotional abuse. I had a "flash-temper" during their formative years. My children never knew if I'd be home in the evenings or out on the town, whether I'd be sober or drunk, or whether I had a job or was unemployed. Perhaps their inability to predict my behavior or mood(s) left them confused and disoriented.

My mother was normal, as were my grandparents on both sides. On the other side, my paternal father was both an alcoholic and a philanderer, a mirror image of myself. Our stepfather was both mentally and physically abusive during my formative years. By the time I was sixteen, he mellowed out and we became close friends.

Heredity could have played a role. I never knew my biological father, so his conduct couldn't have had much of an impact. However, my stepfather's extreme mental and physical abuse during my formative years might have altered my natural emotional state — I just don't know; I am not a professional. Since six of the seven children experienced emotional disorders, I am inclined to believe his behavior towards us left lasting psychological scars. Our family was dysfunctional, and still is today.

Making Sense of God

As a youth, I attended a Baptist church with my mother. I attended a Catholic university, but rarely went to Mass. Both the Baptists and Catholics adhere to rigid doctrines. Either you're Baptist, or you're going to hell. Churchgoers, I noticed, were generally fakes. They'd recite the verses, but they didn't walk the walk. Religion to them was a one-day-a-week event, not a way of life. Today, I am not loyal to any one "church."

All Western religions address similar issues using very different methods. The central theme of Western denominations include a God and an afterlife. What they don't agree on is who gets to see God, who goes to heaven. This seemingly inconsequential difference of views has extracted from the world trillions of dollars, millions of lives and an immeasurable amount of human suffering.

Prior to my NDE, I saw the universality of religions — the core belief — as being an acknowledgment of man's own immortality and his desire to live eternally. Post-NDE, I developed a metaphysical view of the world and mankind. I see man as a small part of an expansive universe. My universe is the embodiment of God Himself. He is the body and humans are the specialized microscopic cells which service the body. We are the worker-ants. We each have a specific mission to fulfill if the body is to remain healthy. We must treat others with dignity and respect. We must procreate in order to provide a continuous supply of healthy cells for the Body. God is within each of us and we are within God. At some point in the future, we will all "live as one."

God was at one time an abstraction to me. Today I know beyond a shadow of a doubt that He's a certainty. He was omnipresent while I suffocated beneath the pile of silage. What I saw and felt forever changed my life, my values and my belief system. No longer do I fear death, it's now a transformation I anticipate with open arms. I yearn to return to the state of euphoria, to return to the "light" at the end of the brilliantly illuminated tunnel.

One change I did take notice of was my ability to sense the essence of what is going to happen in the future, the ability to quickly grasp the intentions of others, and to a lesser extent, occurrences of the past. A person can begin talking about an issue and I can finish the sentence in my head faster than he/she can verbalize it — then I get irritated because the individual seems to be belaboring the point. Wife number two, Leigh, once asked me what was in one of my Christmas packages. Within a few seconds, I told her "it is a brown pin-striped suit, the 'pins' being orange." She never asked me to do that again. I don't wear a watch - I intuitively know the time, give or take a few minutes. Although I never actually receive a command, or compulsion to take specific action, I am gently nudged in one direction or another.

Stock picking is a good example. First, I get an urge to read and/or research a given market, or a certain corporation, or specific commodities; then I react by listening to business news and reading related articles. Sixty to seventy percent of the time, my intuition is spot on. Other times, it just appears to me that I was "in the right place at the right time."

According to Edgar Mitchell, a member of the Institute of Noetic Sciences organization and the sixth man to walk on the moon, intuition (extra-sensory perception) is a sixth sense — something we all have, but few of us use it often enough to keep atrophy from destroying it. Like other sensory functions, such as sight, hearing, and smell, precognition must be used on a regular basis — "use it or lose it."

To paraphrase a Buddhist belief ...the attainment of (psychic) powers is a minor advantage of no value in itself for progress toward liberation. Others say psychic abilities are an impediment and lead to an enhanced sense of self-esteem. To me ESP is simply another tool to be used in one's day-to-day activities. I have discovered that precognitive abilities should not be used for self-aggrandizement, such as attempting to change the outcome of an event, or for a selfish advantage over another. These things are best left to God.

Today I am less responsive to the opinions of others; I dance to the beat of a different drummer. I'm free to be who and what I truly am. Quite simply, I don't give a shit if they approve or disapprove of me or my actions; I answer to God and God alone. I've a much greater feeling of self-acceptance, self-confidence and self-worth.

Suffice it to say, my experience with death was enlightening. "Ye shall know the truth and the truth will set you free."

Bottom of the Ninth

Here I sit in the twilight of my life, writing my memoir, with no significant other in my life. My children don't call me, let alone visit. My ex-wives are more likely to communicate with me than my children. At 66, women I want don't want me. Women that want me, I don't want. I know better than to cohabitate with anyone. If my previous behavior is any indicator, I'll eventually disappoint them — it's my nature.

As I slide into "home-base," I realize it has been one hell of a ride, but at the expense of others. I've been successful. My life has been beautiful, filled with fun, full of spirituality and bliss. But my conduct left a broad swath of destruction and mental anguish in its wake. I'll remain forever remorseful for those I harmed or hurt along the way. I trust God will forgive me — He knows I cannot forgive myself. I wake each morning with a simple prayer.

"God, please put someone in my life I can help."

The End

APPENDIX A

What is Bipolar Depression?

- Depressed mood most of the day; feeling sad or empty, tearful
- Significant loss of interest or pleasure in activities that used to be enjoyable
- Significant weight loss (when not dieting) or weight gain; decrease or increase in appetite
- Difficulty sleeping or sleeping too much
- Agitation or slowing down of thoughts and reduction of physical movements
- Fatigue or loss of energy
- Feelings of worthlessness or inappropriate guilt
- Poor concentration or having difficulty making decisions
- Thinking about death or suicide

From Diagnostic and Statistical Manual of Mental Disorders, Fourth Edition Text Revision

What is a Bipolar Mania?

- Grandiosity
- Decreased need for sleep
- Pressured speech
- Racing thoughts
- Distractibility
- Tendency to engage in behavior that could have serious consequences, such as spending recklessly or inappropriate sexual encounters
- Excess energy

From www.About.com

References

Books:
Diagnostic and Statistical Manual of Mental Disorders DSM-IV-TR,
Fourth Edition, (Text Revision), by American Psychiatric Association.

Websites:
www.About.Com/Health Bipolar I/
www.dead-frog.com/comedians/jokes/bill_cosby/
www.buddhistchannel.tv/index.php
The Writer

www.ingramcontent.com/pod-product-compliance
Lightning Source LLC
Chambersburg PA
CBHW022358280326
41935CB00007B/224